D1304115

saturday style

casual
knits
for
weekend
wear

Doreen L. Marquart

Martingale®
& COMPANY

Credits

President & CEO – Tom Wierzbicki

Editor in Chief – Mary V. Green

Managing Editor – Tina Cook

Developmental Editor – Karen Costello Soltys

Technical Editor – Robin Strobel

Copy Editor – Liz McGehee

Design Director – Stan Green

Production Manager – Regina Girard

Illustrator – Laurel Strand

Cover & Text Designer – Shelly Garrison

Photographer – Brent Kane

Mission Statement

Dedicated to providing quality products
and service to inspire creativity.

Saturday Style: Casual Knits for Weekend Wear
© 2010 by Doreen L. Marquart

Martingale & Company®
20205 144th Ave. NE
Woodinville, WA 98072-8478 USA
www.martingale-pub.com

Printed in China
15 14 13 12 11 10   8 7 6 5 4 3 2 1

Library of Congress Cataloging-in-Publication Data is available upon request.

ISBN: 978-1-56477-918-2

DEDICATION

To my dear friends Barb Becker, Karen Kuckenbecker, Joan LeClair, and Joan Merrifield. Thank you for always being there for me, in my knitting life as well as my nonknitting life. Thank you for letting me bounce ideas off of you, for letting me know when you agree and when you think I am way off base. Thank you for allowing me to vent to you . . . and not getting up and walking away! Thank you for kidnapping me for a day or two when you can see that I am reaching the total stressed-out point. We've had some great knitting and nonknitting adventures together. I can't wait for our next one!

ACKNOWLEDGMENTS

I'd like to thank:

My wonderful customers, who are first and foremost my friends. I just happen to supply you with the materials needed to serve your addiction to knitting!

The yarn companies who graciously provided beautiful yarns to bring the designs in this book to life. It's great to have such wonderful fibers to work with.

Martingale & Company, for allowing me so much freedom in sharing my creative designs with the knitting world. Once again, it's been a pleasure to work with everyone.

My technical editor, Robin Strobel, for guiding me through the editing process and making this book become a reality.

CONTENTS

INTRODUCTION 7

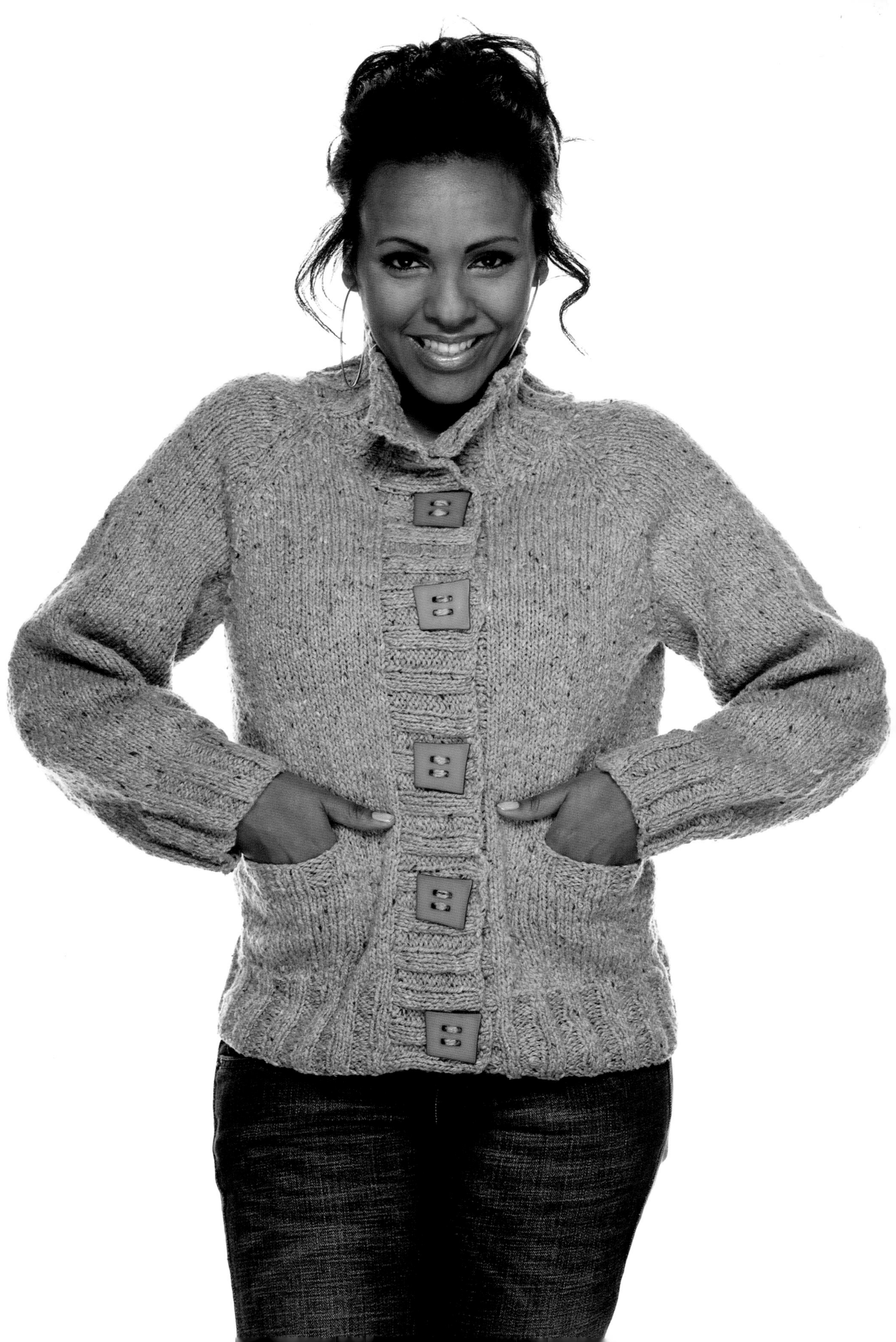

INTRODUCTION

I've always loved to knit. In fact, I can't remember a time when I didn't knit. I'm very fortunate that I've been able to turn what started as a childhood hobby into a livelihood. I can now share my love of knitting not only with customers at my shop, Needles 'n Pins Yarn Shoppe, but also with the rest of the knitting world through my books.

This sequel to *Saturday Sweaters* came about because I still had many designs living in my head that wanted to come to life. While they're a little more involved and require slightly more skills and techniques than those in *Saturday Sweaters*, they're still sweaters that the not-so-advanced knitter will feel confident tackling. And, since many of the designs take a different approach to construction than is common, even experienced knitters will find them interesting to make. Sometimes knitting a sweater is like putting a puzzle together; it's always fascinating to see how the project evolves.

While working on this book, I was once again reminded what an important part knitting plays in my life. It's my friend, my companion, my therapy. I turn to knitting when life hands me a challenge. It calms me, settles me, and soothes my soul. As I sit and knit, I'm able to put the happenings of my life in perspective and gather the strength I need.

I hope you enjoy making these sweaters as much as I've enjoyed bringing them to life. And, as you sit and knit, I hope that you, too, can find the peace and solace in knitting that only a knitter understands!

SWING IN STYLE CARDIGAN

This cardigan is knit entirely in one piece starting from the collar. The only finishing you have to do is sewing on the pockets and weaving in the ends—a knitter's dream! Add to that a pretty, bulky-weight yarn that knits up fast and you'll be done in no time. The comfortable, slightly flared styling of this cardigan is sure to make it one of your favorite chill chasers.

Skill Level: Easy ◐■☐◁

Finished Bust Measurement: 36 (40, 44, 48, 52, 56)"
Finished Length: 24 (25, 25, 26, 26, 27)"
Sleeve Drop: 8 (8½, 9½, 10, 11, 11)"

MATERIALS

Yarn: 7 (8, 10, 12, 13, 15) skeins of Nature Wool Chunky Multy from Araucania (100% wool; 3.5 oz/100 g; 132 yds/120 m) in color 207, or approx 900 (1050, 1250, 1475, 1700, 1980) yds of bulky-weight yarn (5)

Needles: Size 10 (6 mm) circular needles (16" and 29" or longer) or size required to attain gauge, size 10 double-pointed needles

Notions: Stitch markers; stitch holders; 3 buttons, approx 1" diameter

Gauge: 16 sts and 19 rows = 4" in St st

SEED STITCH
Row 1: K1, P1 across row or rnd.
Row 2: Purl the knit sts and knit the purl sts from previous row as they face you.

COLLAR AND YOKE

Beg at neck edge and with 16" circular needle, CO 58 (58, 64, 64, 70, 70) sts.

Work 6 rows in St st.

Work 6 rows in seed st.

These 12 rows form collar. Beg yoke and pm as follows to divide in sections:

Row 1 (RS): CO 6 sts for front band, K8 (8, 9, 9, 10, 10) for front, pm, K1 for seam st, pm, K11 (11, 12, 12, 13, 13) for sleeve, pm, K1 for seam st, pm, K16 (16, 18, 18, 20, 20) for back, pm, K1 for seam st, pm, K11 (11, 12, 12, 13, 13) for sleeve, pm, K1 for seam st, pm, K8 (8, 9, 9, 10, 10) for front, pm, CO 6 sts for front band—70 (70, 76, 76, 82, 82) total sts.

Working front band sts (first and last 6 sts) in seed st throughout entire sweater, cont yoke as follows:

Row 2: Purl.

Row 3: *Knit to marker, M1, sm, K1, sm, M1, rep from * 3 more times, knit to end of row (8-st inc).

Row 4: Purl.

Row 5 (first buttonhole row): Work in patt to last 4 sts, BO 2 sts, work in patt to end of row.

Row 6 (second buttonhole row): Work 2 sts in patt, CO 2 sts, work in patt to end of row.

Rep rows 3 and 4, keeping front bands in seed st, working 2nd buttonhole when front band measures 4" and 3rd buttonhole when band measures 7". Switch to longer circular needle when enough sts to do so.

Cont working in patt with no more buttonholes to 230 (230, 244, 244, 258, 258) sts, ending with RS row. Sections should contain the foll number of sts:

Front bands: 6 sts each.

Fronts: 28 (28, 30, 30, 32, 32) sts each.

Sleeves: 51 (51, 54, 54, 57, 57) sts each.

Back: 56 (56, 60, 60, 64, 64) sts.

Seams: 4 sts total.

Dividing for fronts and back (WS): Removing markers as you come to them, work in patt across 86 (86, 91, 91, 96, 96) sts, place preceding 51 (51, 54, 54, 57, 57) sts on holder or spare yarn for sleeve, work in patt across 109 (109, 116, 116, 123, 123) sts, place preceding 51 (51, 54, 54, 57, 57) sts on holder or spare yarn for 2nd sleeve, work rem 35 (35, 37, 37, 39, 39) sts in patt.

BODY

Foundation row (RS): Work 35 (35, 37, 37, 39, 39) sts in patt, pm, CO 11 (19, 23, 31, 35, 43) sts, pm, work 58 (58, 62, 62, 66, 66) sts in patt, pm, CO 11 (19, 23, 31, 35, 43) sts, pm, work rem 35 (35, 37, 37, 39, 39) sts in patt—150 (166, 182, 198, 214, 230) total sts.

Work even in patt until body measure 2" from underarm, ending with WS row.

Inc row: *Work in patt to 1 st before marker, L1 (see page 74), sm, L1, rep from * 3 more times, work in patt to end of row (8-st inc).

Cont in patt, working inc row every 2" for a total of 6 times. Work even on 198 (214, 230, 246, 262, 278) sts until body measures 22 (23, 23, 24, 24, 25)" or 2" less than desired finished length, ending with WS row.

Bottom border: Work 2" in seed st, ending with WS row. BO in patt.

SLEEVES

With RS facing you and 16" circular needle, PU 12 (20, 24, 32, 36, 44) sts along underarm section, pm of a different color after first 6 (10, 12, 16, 18, 22) sts to denote beg of rnd. K1 from sleeve sts, pm, K49 (49, 52, 52, 55, 55) from sleeve sts, pm, knit rem st from sleeve sts—63 (71, 78, 86, 93, 101) total sts. Knit to end of rnd. You've knit an extra row on half the underarm stitches but this won't be noticeable.

Rnd 1: Knit.

Rnd 2: Knit to 2 sts before marker, K2tog, sm, knit to next marker, sm, ssk, knit to end of rnd.

Rep rnds 1 and 2 until 51 (51, 54, 54, 57, 57) sts rem, switching to dpns when necessary. Remove all markers except beg-of-rnd marker and work even until sleeve measures 18½" from underarm or 1½" less than desired finished sleeve length. Work 6 rnds in seed st followed by 6 knit rnds. BO.

DOREEN'S TIP

If you end up with little holes where the underarm stitches were picked up, simply use the yarn tail or an extra piece of yarn to weave around those stitches and tighten them. These holes sometimes result after stitches have been on holders.

POCKETS (MAKE 2)

With shorter circular needle or dpns, CO 19 (19, 21, 21, 23, 23) sts.

Work 6 rows in seed st.

Cont in St st until pocket measures 4½ (4½, 5, 5, 5½, 5½)" from beg, ending with WS row. BO.

FINISHING

Sew buttons to left front band to correspond to buttonholes on right front band. Sew pockets to front sections, placing bottom edge of pocket just above seed-st border of sweater body, and side edge of pocket just inside inc line of corresponding front section. Weave in ends.

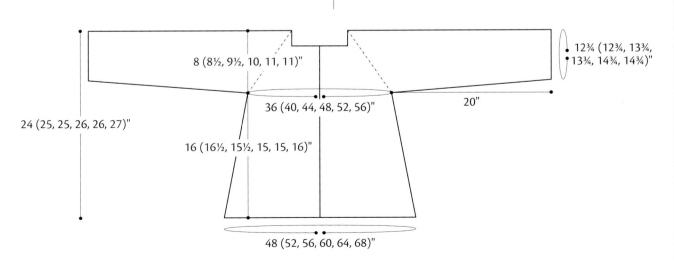

8 (8½, 9½, 10, 11, 11)"

12¾ (12¾, 13¾, 13¾, 14¾, 14¾)"

36 (40, 44, 48, 52, 56)"

20"

24 (25, 25, 26, 26, 27)"

16 (16½, 15½, 15, 15, 16)"

48 (52, 56, 60, 64, 68)"

DROP-SHOULDER TEE

This is an easy-to-knit summer top, and you are definitely going to want more than one! The stitch pattern adds interest yet isn't too busy to use with multicolored yarns. While I chose a hand-painted cotton, the pattern stitch is equally attractive in a solid color.

Skill Level: Easy ◀■□▷

Finished Bust Measurement: 36 (40½, 45½, 48, 52½)"

Finished Length: 22 (22½, 23, 23½, 24)"

Armhole Opening: 7 (7½, 8, 8½, 9)"

MATERIALS

Yarn: 3 (3, 4, 4, 5) skeins of Ulmo Multy from Araucania (100% cotton; 100 g; 202 yds) in color 702, or 550 (625, 700, 800, 900) yds of lightweight (DK) yarn (3)

Needles: Size 5 (3.75 mm) needles or size required to attain gauge, size 5 circular needle (16" long)

Notions: Stitch markers, locking-type stitch markers, stitch holders

Gauge: 20 sts and 32 rows = 4" in pattern stitch

BACK

Beg at lower back and with straight needles, CO 90 (102, 114, 120, 132) sts.

Row 1 (RS): K2, P2, *K4, P2, rep from * to last 2 sts, K2.

Row 2: Purl.

Rep rows 1 and 2 for patt. Work in patt until back measures 21 (21½, 22, 22½, 23)" from beg or 1" less than desired finished length, ending with WS row.

Back Neck Shaping

Next row (RS): Work in patt 26 (32, 37, 40, 45) sts. Attach another ball of yarn, work across next 38 (38, 40, 40, 42) sts and place them on holder, work rem 26 (32, 37, 40, 45) sts.

Working both sides at same time and using separate yarn balls, cont in patt while dec 1 st at each side of neck edge every RS row until 24 (30, 35, 38, 43) sts rem on each side, ending with WS row.

Recommended dec: K2tog at left neck edge, ssk at right neck edge.

Work even until total length of back is 22 (22½, 23, 23½, 24)" from CO edge. Place sts on separate holders to be joined later to front shoulders.

FRONT

Work same as back until piece measures 17 (17½, 18, 18½, 19)" from beg or 5" less than total length of back, ending with WS row.

Front Neck Shaping

Next row (RS): Work in patt across 30 (36, 41, 44, 49) sts, attach 2nd yarn ball, work in patt across next 30 (30, 32, 32, 34) sts and place these sts on holder. Work rem 30 (36, 41, 44, 49) sts in patt.

Working both sides at same time and using separate balls of yarn, cont in patt while dec 1 st at each side of neck edge *every RS row* until 24 (30, 35, 38, 43) sts rem on each side. Work even until front measures same length as back, ending with WS row.

Recommended dec: K2tog at left neck edge, ssk at right neck edge.

FINISHING

Join front to back at shoulders using 3-needle BO (page 76). Measure 7 (7½, 8, 8½, 9)" down from shoulder seam and pm along sides of garment. Sew side seams, beg at bottom edge and ending at markers.

Armhole Bands

With RS facing you and circular needle, beg at lower edge of opening, PU 76 (80, 84, 90, 96) sts around armhole opening. Pm to denote beg of rnd.

Rnds 1 and 3: Purl.

Rnds 2 and 4: Knit.

BO pw.

Neckband

With RS facing you and circular needle, PU neckband sts as follows: PU 6 sts along side of right back neck edge, K38 (38, 40, 40, 42) from back holder, PU 6 sts along side of left back neck edge, PU 26 sts along side of left front neck edge, K30 (30, 32, 32, 34) from front neck holder, PU 26 sts along side of right front neck edge—132 (132, 136, 136, 140) total sts.

Pm to denote beg of rnd.

Rnds 1 and 3: Purl.

Rnd 2: K5, K2tog, K36 (36, 38, 38, 40); K2tog, K30, K2tog; K28 (28, 30, 30, 32), K2tog, K25—128 (128, 132, 132, 136) sts.

Rnd 4: K4, K2tog, K36 (36, 38, 38, 40); K2tog, K28, K2tog; K28 (28, 30, 30, 32), K2tog, K24—124 (124, 128, 128, 132) sts.

BO pw. Weave in all ends.

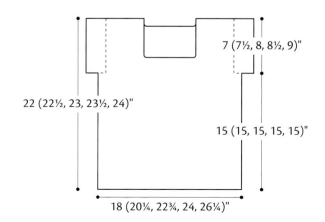

7 (7½, 8, 8½, 9)"

22 (22½, 23, 23½, 24)"

15 (15, 15, 15, 15)"

18 (20¼, 22¾, 24, 26¼)"

SCALLOPED-EDGE TUNIC

This tunic is knit in one piece from the bottom up to the armholes. Sleeves are picked up and knit down, making for a garment that requires no seaming. Just knit, bind off, weave in ends, and wear!

Skill Level: Intermediate ◼◼◼◻

Finished Bust Measurement:
36 (40, 43¾, 47½, 51½)"

Finished Length: 27 (27½, 28, 28½, 29)"

Sleeve Drop: 9 (9½, 10, 10½, 11)"

MATERIALS

Yarn: 3 (4, 4, 4, 5) skeins of Wool Twist from Happy Hands Yarn (100% wool; 8 oz/400 g; 560 yds/510 m) in color Dust in the Wind, or approx 1500 (1700, 1925, 2175, 2450) yds of lightweight (DK) yarn 🧶③

Needles: Size 6 (4 mm) circular needles (16" and 29" long) or size required to attain gauge, size 6 double-pointed needles

Notions: Stitch markers, stitch holders

Gauge: 21 sts and 28 rows = 4" in St st

BODY

Beg at bottom edge and with longer circular needle, CO 250 (270, 290, 310, 330) sts. Join, being careful not to twist, and pm to denote beg of rnd. Knit 1 rnd. Purl 1 rnd.

Beg patt as follows:
Rnd 1: *K7, YO, K7 (8, 9, 10, 11), ssk, K2tog, K7 (8, 9, 10, 11), YO, rep from * around.

Rnd 2: *P7, K18 (20, 22, 24, 26), rep from * around.

Rep rnds 1 and 2 until piece measures 2" from beg, ending with rnd 1.

First dec rnd: *P3, P2 tog, P2, K18 (20, 22, 24, 26), rep from * around—240 (260, 280, 300, 320) sts.

Cont in patt as follows:
Rnd 1: *K6, YO, K7 (8, 9, 10, 11), ssk, K2tog, K7 (8, 9, 10, 11), YO, rep from * around.

Rnd 2: *P6, K18 (20, 22, 24, 26), rep from * around.

Rep rnds 1 and 2 until piece measures 5", ending with rnd 1.

Second dec rnd: *P2, P2tog, P2, K18 (20, 22, 24, 26), rep from * around—230 (250, 270, 290, 310) sts.

Cont in patt as follows:
Rnd 1: *K5, YO, K7 (8, 9, 10, 11), ssk, K2tog, K7 (8, 9, 10, 11), YO, rep from * around.

Rnd 2: *P5, K18 (20, 22, 24, 26), rep from * around.

Rep rnds 1 and 2 until piece measures 8", ending with rnd 1.

Third dec rnd: *P2, P2tog, P1, K18 (20, 22, 24, 26), rep from * around—220 (240, 260, 280, 300) sts.

Cont in patt as follows:
Rnd 1: *K4, YO, K7 (8, 9, 10, 11), ssk, K2tog, K7 (8, 9, 10, 11), YO, rep from * around.

Rnd 2: *P4, K18 (20, 22, 24, 26), rep from * around.

Rep rnds 1 and 2 until piece measures 11", ending with rnd 1.

Fourth dec rnd: *P1, P2tog, P1, K18 (20, 22, 24, 26), rep from * around—210 (230, 250, 270, 280) sts.

Cont in patt as follows:
Rnd 1: *K3, YO, K7 (8, 9, 10, 11), ssk, K2tog, K7 (8, 9, 10, 11), YO, rep from * around.

Rnd 2: *P3, K18 (20, 22, 24, 26), rep from * around.

Rep rnds 1 and 2 until piece measures 14", ending with rnd 1.

Fifth dec rnd: *P1, P2tog, K18 (20, 22, 24, 26), rep from * around—200 (220, 240, 260, 280) sts.

Cont in patt as follows:

Rnd 1: *K2, YO, K7 (8, 9, 10, 11), ssk, K2tog, K7 (8, 9, 10, 11), YO, rep from * around.

Rnd 2: *P2, K18 (20, 22, 24, 26), rep from * around.

Rep rnds 1 and 2 until piece measures 17", ending with rnd 1.

Sixth dec rnd: *P2tog, K18 (20, 22, 24, 26), rep from * around—190 (210, 230, 250, 270) sts.

Cont in patt as follows:

Rnds 1, 3, and 5: Knit.

Rnds 2, 4, and 6: Purl.

DIVIDING FOR FRONT AND BACK

K10 (11, 12, 13, 14) sts, place preceding 19 (21, 23, 25, 27) sts on holder to be used later for left underarm, K76 (84, 92, 100, 108) and place on 2nd holder for front, K19 (21, 23, 25, 27) and place on 3rd holder for right underarm, K76 (84, 92, 100, 108) for back, leaving these sts on needle.

BACK

Beg with WS row, work back and forth in St st until back measures 9 (9½, 10, 10½, 11)" from dividing rnd, ending with WS row.

Divide sts on 3 holders as follows:
First and third holders: 25 (28, 30, 33, 36) sts each.

Second holder: 26 (28, 32, 34, 36) sts.

FRONT

Return front sts to needle. With WS facing you, attach yarn. Work as for back until piece measures 5 (5½, 6, 6½, 7)". End on WS row.

Neck Shaping

K30 (33, 35, 38, 41), place next 16 (18, 22, 24, 26) sts on holder for neckband, attach 2nd skein of yarn and knit across rem 30 (33, 35, 38, 41) sts.

Working both sides at same time, dec 1 st at each side of neck every RS row until 25 (28, 30, 33, 36) sts rem.

Suggested dec: For a nice smooth look, K2tog on left neck edge and ssk on right neck edge.

Work even on rem sts until front measures same as back, ending with WS row.

Join front shoulder sts to back shoulder sts using 3-needle BO (page 76).

LEFT SLEEVE

With RS facing you, attach yarn. Using 16" needle, K9 (10, 11, 12, 13) left underarm sts from first holder, pm to denote beg of rnd. K8 (9, 10, 11, 12), K2tog, pm, PU 96 (100, 106, 110, 116) sts around armhole opening, pm, K9 (10, 11, 12, 13) to finish rnd—114 (120, 128, 134, 142) sts.

Gusset Shaping

Rnd 1: Knit to 2 sts before marker, K2tog, sm, knit to next marker, sm, ssk, knit to end of rnd.

Rnd 2: Knit.

Rep rnds 1 and 2 until 1 st rem between beg-of-rnd marker and second marker and between third marker and beg-of-rnd marker. At this point all markers except beg-of-rnd marker may be removed—98 (102, 108, 112, 118) total sts.

Body of Sleeve

Cont in St st, dec 1 st at beg and end of every 5 rnds until 54 (58, 60, 64, 68) sts rem.

Work even until sleeve measures 19" from PU rnd or 1" less than desired finished length.

Recommended dec: At beg of rnds, K1, K2tog. At end of rnds, knit to last 3 sts, ssk, K1.

Cuff

Rnds 1, 3, 5, and 7: Purl.

Rnds 2, 4, 6, and 8: Knit.

Rnd 9: BO pw.

RIGHT SLEEVE

With RS facing you, sl 9 (10, 11, 12, 13) sts from st holder to 16" circular needle, pm to denote beg of rnd.

K8 (9, 10, 11, 12), K2 tog (all sts on holder worked), pm, PU 96 (100, 106, 110, 116) sts around armhole opening, pm, knit to beg of rnd marker.

Work gusset shaping, body of sleeve, and cuff as for left sleeve.

NECKBAND

With RS facing you and 16" circular needle, beg at left shoulder, PU 26 sts on left front edge, K16 (18, 22, 24, 26) from front holder, PU 26 sts on right front edge, K26 (28, 32, 34, 36) from back holder, pm to denote beg of rnd—94 (98, 106, 110, 114) total sts.

Rnd 1: Purl.

Rnd 2: Knit.

BO pw.

FINISHING

Weave in ends. Block, pinning bottom edges to form nice, sharp points.

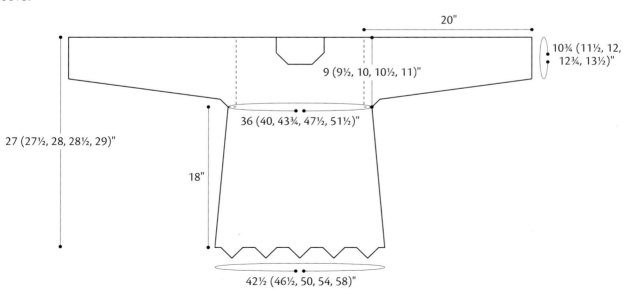

20"

10¾ (11½, 12, 12¾, 13½)"

9 (9½, 10, 10½, 11)"

36 (40, 43¾, 47½, 51½)"

27 (27½, 28, 28½, 29)"

18"

42½ (46½, 50, 54, 58)"

SIDE-BUTTON CARDIGAN

Who says that a cardigan has to button down the center? Unique buttons add flair to this easy-to-knit cardigan that can be worn with jeans for casual days or dressed up for special occasions.

Skill Level: Easy ◖■□▷

Finished Bust Measurement:	36 (40, 44, 48, 52)"
Finished Length:	23¼"
Sleeve Drop:	8¼ (8¾, 9½, 10¼, 10¼)"
Sleeve Length:	19½ (19½, 20, 20½, 20½)"

MATERIALS

Yarn: 9 (11, 12, 14, 16) skeins of Autunno from DiVe (100% merino wool; 1¾ oz/50 g; 98 yds/90 m) in color 34048, or approx 850 (990, 1145, 1325, 1530) yds of bulky-weight yarn ⓹

Needles: Size 9 (5.5 mm) circular needles (16" and 29" or longer) or size required to attain gauge, size 9 double-pointed needles, spare circular needle of same size or smaller

Notions: Stitch markers; stitch holders; 6 buttons, approx 1¼" diameter

Gauge: 16 sts and 22 rows = 4" in St st

BODY

Beg at lower edge and with longer circular needle, CO 152 (168, 184, 200, 216) sts.

Row 1 (RS): K9 for front buttonhole band, pm, K48 (52, 56, 60, 64) for right front, pm, K72 (80, 88, 96, 104) for back, pm, K14 (18, 22, 26, 30) for left front, pm, K9 for front button band.

Rows 2–4: Knit.

Row 5 (first buttonhole row): K4, BO 2 sts, knit to end of row.

Row 6 (second buttonhole row): Knit until 4 sts rem on left needle, CO 2 sts, K4.

Row 7 (RS): Knit.

Row 8 (WS): K9, purl to last 9 sts, K9.

Rep rows 7 and 8 (first and last 9 sts are garter-st bands, body is St st), working buttonholes on appropriate rows, ending with row 83 (79, 75, 71, 71). Piece should measure approx 15 (14½, 13¾, 13, 13)" from beg.

BUTTONHOLE SPACING

Since the button and buttonhole bands are knit at the same time as the body, buttonholes need to be worked as you go. You will need to keep track of rows and make buttonholes (repeat rows 5 and 6) on the following rows:

Rows 5–6	Rows 29–30	Rows 53–54
Rows 77–78	Rows 101–102	Rows 125–126

There should be 12 garter-stitch "ridges" between each set of buttonhole rows.

Armhole Border

Rows 84 (80, 76, 72, 72); 86 (82, 78, 74, 74); and 88 (84, 80, 76, 76) (WS): K9 for button band, P4 (8, 11, 15, 18) for left front, K20 (20, 22, 22, 24) for armhole border, P52 (60, 66, 74, 80) for back, K20 (20, 22, 22, 24) for armhole border, P38 (42, 45, 49, 52) for right front, K9 for buttonhole band.

Rows 85 (81, 77, 73, 73) and 87 (83, 79, 75, 75): Knit.

RIGHT FRONT

Row 89 (85, 81, 77, 77) (RS): K52 (56, 59, 63, 66). Place rem sts on spare circular needle. You will be working back and forth.

Next row: K5, P38 (42, 45, 49, 52), K9.

Cont working front in St st, keeping 5-st armhole band and 9-st buttonhole band in garter st as estab. Work even, making buttonholes on appropriate rows, ending with row 110.

Neck Shaping

Work 13 sts in estab patt. Attach 2nd ball of yarn, K17 and place these sts on holder to be used later for neckband, work rem 22 (26, 29, 33, 36) sts in estab patt.

Working both sides at same time and using separate balls of yarn, cont in patt while dec 1 st at each side of neck edge every RS row for a total of 4 times.

Left shoulder—9 sts rem.

Right shoulder—18 (22, 25, 29, 32) sts rem.

Recommended dec: K2tog at left neck edge, ssk at right neck edge.

Work even, ending on row 128. Front should measure about 23". BO left shoulder sts. Cut yarn on right shoulder sts and place these sts on holder.

BACK

With RS facing you, sl next 10 (10, 12, 12, 14) sts from spare circular needle to st holder to be used later for underarm. Attach yarn, K62 (70, 76, 84, 90) on "working" needle. Leave sts rem on spare needle to be worked later. Keeping first and last 5 sts in garter st for armhole borders, work even in St st, ending with row 128. Cut yarn. Divide sts on 3 holders as follows:

First and third holders: 18 (22, 25, 29, 32) sts each.

Second holder: 26 sts

LEFT FRONT

With RS facing you, sl next 10 (10, 12, 12, 14) sts from spare circular needle to st holder to be used later for underarm. Attach yarn and knit rem 18 (22, 25, 29, 32) sts back on "working" needle. Cont in St st, working 5 st buttonhole band and 9 st armhole band in garter st as estab, ending with row 128.

Join front to back shoulders using 3-needle BO (page 76).

SLEEVES

Sleeves are worked in the round. With RS facing you, sl 10 (10, 12, 12, 14) sts from one underarm holder to 16" circular needle, pm after 5 (5, 6, 6, 7) sts to denote beg of rnd. (Beg-of-rnd marker should be different color than ones placed in next step to mark decs.) PU additional 64 (68, 72, 76, 80) sts around armhole as follows:

PU and *purl* 1 st, pm, PU and *purl* 62 (66, 70, 74, 78) sts, pm, PU and *purl* 1 st, knit to end of rnd—74 (78, 84, 88, 94) sts.

Knit 4 rnds even.

PICK UP LIKE A PRO!

For best results, when picking up stitches around an armhole, insert the needle through the bumps of the garter stitches along the armhole edge of the body. (To attain the required number of stitches, you'll need to go through a few of the "valleys" also.) See "Picking Up Stitches" on page 75.

Underarm dec rnd: Knit to 2 sts before first dec marker, K2tog, sm, knit to next dec marker, sm, ssk, knit to end of rnd.

Work in St st, dec every 4th rnd until all underarm sts are dec. You should have beg-of-rnd marker, with 1 st between dec markers on either side—64 (68, 72, 76, 80) sts.

Knit 4 rounds even, removing dec markers.

Sleeve dec rnd: K1, K2tog, knit to last 3 sts, ssk, K1.

Cont working in St st, dec every 5th rnd until 34 (36, 38, 42, 46) sts rem, switching to dpn when necessary. Work even until sleeve measures 19 (19, 19½, 20, 20)" or ½" less than desired finished length.

Cuff

Rnds 1 and 3: Purl.

Rnds 2 and 4: Knit.

BO in purl.

NECKBAND

With RS facing you, PU 20 sts along left side of front neck, K17 sts from center front holder, PU 20 sts along right side of front neck, K26 from back neck holder—83 total sts.

Rows 1 and 3 (WS): Knit.

Row 2: K19, K2tog, K15, K2tog, knit to end of row.

Row 4: K19, K2tog, K13, K2tog, knit to end of row.

BO in knit on WS.

FINISHING

Weave in all ends. Attach buttons on button band to correspond to buttonholes.

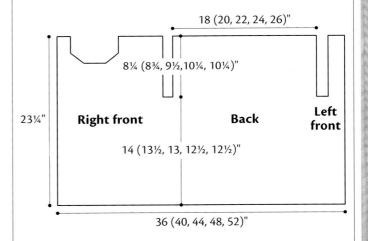

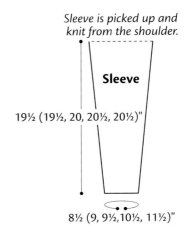

Sleeve is picked up and knit from the shoulder.

SIDE-BUTTON CARDIGAN

23

RASPBERRY MOCHA CARDIGAN

Sometimes it's not about how fast a sweater knits up. Sometimes it's about the process and letting the beauty of the stitches, created in this cardigan by using small needles and fine-weight yarn, shine through. Why not knit a sweater using one of the many gorgeous color combinations from Claudia Hand Painted Yarns, and then knit a second one from a solid? Either way, you'll have a wonderful lightweight cardigan for cooler temperatures.

Skill Level: Intermediate ◖■■▭

Finished Bust Measurement: 36 (40, 44, 48, 52)"

Finished Length: 25"

Sleeve Drop: 9 (9, 10, 10, 11)"

MATERIALS

Yarn: 11 (13, 14, 16, 18) skeins of Claudia Fingering Yarn by Claudia Hand Painted Yarns (100% wool; 1.75 oz/100 g; 175 yds/159 m) in color Cabin Fever, or approx 1875 (2120, 2400, 2700, 3050) yds of fingering-weight (super fine) yarn (2)

Needles: Size 3 (3.25 mm) circular needles (16", 24", and 32" or longer) or size required to attain gauge, size 3 double-pointed needles

Notions: Stitch markers; stitch holders; 6 buttons, ¾" to 1" diameter

Gauge: 28 sts and 36 rows = 4" in St st

Since the front bands are knit at the same time as the fronts, you need to work buttonhole rows as you go. Work buttonhole rows when the piece measures ½", 4¼", 8", 11¾", 15½", and 19¼". If you alter the finished length, remember you have to alter buttonhole placement, too.

First buttonhole row (RS): Work 5 sts in patt, BO next 2 sts, work in patt to end of row.

Second buttonhole row: Work in patt until 5 sts rem on left needle, CO 2 sts, work in patt to end of row.

BODY

Beg at lower edge and with longest circular needle, CO 264 (294, 324, 348, 378) sts.

Border patt for body and sleeves:
Row 1 (RS): P2, *sl 1 pw-K1-YO-psso, P4, rep from * to last 4 sts, sl 1 pw-K1-YO-psso, P2.

Row 2: Purl.

Work in border patt for 2 (2½, 2½, 3, 3)", ending with WS row. *(Don't forget to make buttonhole!)*

Border patt for front bands:
Row 1 (RS): P2, sl 1 pw-K1-YO-psso, P4, sl 1 pw-K1-YO-psso, P2.

Row 2: P12.

Keeping first and last 12 sts in border patt for front bands (and working buttonholes at intervals listed), work even in St st until total body of sweater measures 16 (16, 15, 15, 14)", ending with WS row.

Dividing Fronts and Back

K72 (78, 84, 90, 96) (including band sts), place on holder for right front.

K120 (138, 156, 168, 186), leave sts on needle for back.

Place rem 72 (78, 84, 90, 96) sts (including band sts) on holder for left front.

BACK

Working back and forth, cont in St st until armhole opening measures 9 (9, 10, 10, 11)", ending with WS row. Divide sts on holders as follows:

First and third holders: 40 (48, 53, 59, 66) sts each.

Second holder: 40 (42, 50, 50, 54) sts.

RIGHT FRONT

Return right front sts to needle with RS facing you. Attach yarn. Keeping 12 front band sts in border patt as estab and making buttonholes at appropriate places, work in St st 4 (4, 5, 5, 6)" more, ending with WS row.

Neck Shaping

Next row (RS): BO 20 sts, knit to end of row—52 (58, 64, 70, 76) sts rem.

Cont in estab patt while dec 1 st at neck edge every RS row a total of 12 (10, 11, 11, 10) times, ending with WS row—40 (48, 53, 59, 66) sts rem.

Recommended dec: Ssk 1 st from neck edge.

Work even until front measures same as back, ending with WS row. Join right front shoulder to back right shoulder using 3-needle BO (page 76).

LEFT FRONT

Return left front sts to needle. Tie on new ball of yarn. Keeping 12 front band sts in patt, work in St st until piece measures same as right front to neck shaping, ending with RS row.

Neck Shaping

Next row (WS): BO 20 sts, purl to end of row.

Cont in estab patt while dec 1 st at neck edge every RS row a total of 12 (10, 11, 11, 10) times, ending with WS row—40 (48, 53, 59, 66) sts rem.

Recommended dec: K2tog 1 st from neck edge.

Work even until front measures same as back. Join left front shoulder to back left shoulder using 3-needle BO.

SLEEVES

Beg at cuff, CO 66 (72, 72, 78, 78) sts. Work 2" in border patt, ending with WS row. Beg working in St st, inc 1 st at each end of 5th row and every foll 6th row until there are 126 (126, 140, 140, 154) sts.

Recommended inc: M1 after first st of rnd and M1 before last st of rnd.

Work even until sleeve measures 20" from beg or desired finished sleeve length, ending with WS row. BO loosely.

NECKBAND

With RS facing you, PU 49 (51, 53, 53, 57) sts along right front, K40 (42, 50, 50, 54) from back holder, PU 49 (51, 53, 53, 57) sts along left front—138 (144, 156, 156, 168) total sts.

Keeping first and last 12 sts in border patt for front bands, work 1" in garter st, ending with RS row. BO in patt on WS.

FINISHING

Sew sleeve seams. Sew sleeves to body. Weave in loose ends. Sew on buttons to correspond with buttonholes. Block if necessary.

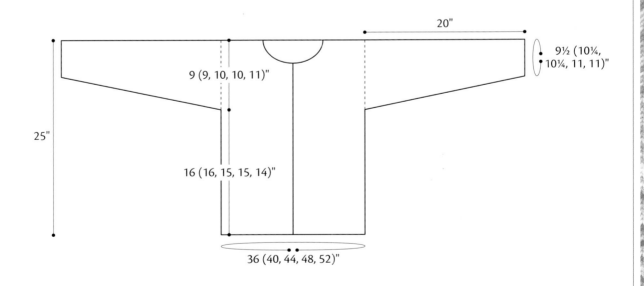

20"

9½ (10¼, 10¼, 11, 11)"

9 (9, 10, 10, 11)"

25"

16 (16, 15, 15, 14)"

36 (40, 44, 48, 52)"

COMFY **CARDIGAN**

The comfy styling of this long cardigan will make you crave chilly days so you can wrap yourself up in the cuddliness of its design and warm yourself up!

Skill Level: Easy ◖■☐◗

Finished Bust Measurement: 36 (40, 44, 48, 52)"

Finished Length: 28 (28½, 29, 29½, 30)"

Sleeve Drop: 9 (9½, 10, 10½, 11)"

MATERIALS

Yarn: 8 (9, 10, 11, 12) skeins of Princess from Schulana (51% merino wool, 30% kid mohair, 18% nylon/elastane; 1.75 oz/50 g; 165 yds/150 m) in color 8, or approx 1320 (1485, 1650, 1815, 1980) yds of medium-weight yarn ⦅**4**⦆

Needles: Size 8 (5 mm) circular needles (16" and 29" or longer) or size required to attain gauge, size 8 (5 mm) double-pointed needles

Notions: Stitch markers, stitch holders

Gauge: 17 sts and 24 rows = 4" in St st

BODY

Beg at bottom and with longer circular needle, CO 160 (176, 192, 208, 224) sts. Knit 4 rows. Beg working in St st, marking row 5 as RS. Cont in St st until piece measures 19" from beg or desired length to armhole, ending with WS row.

Dividing Fronts and Back

K44 (48, 52, 56, 60) and place on holder to be used later for right front.

K72 (80, 88, 96, 104) for back, place rem 44 (48, 52, 56, 60) sts on holder to be used later for left front.

BACK

Cont working in St st until armhole opening measures 9 (9½, 10, 10½, 11)", ending with RS row.

Next row: P24 (28, 31, 34, 37) and place these sts on holder for shoulder, BO next 24 (24, 26, 28, 30) sts, P24 (28, 31, 34, 37) and place these sts on holder for other shoulder.

RIGHT FRONT

Return right front sts to needle. With WS facing you, attach yarn. Beg with a purl row, work in St st until armhole opening measures same as back, ending with RS row.

Next row: P24 (28, 31, 34, 37), place rem 20 (20, 21, 22, 23) sts on holder to be used later for back

neckband. Using 3-needle BO (page 76), join sts on needle to corresponding back shoulder sts.

LEFT FRONT

Return left front sts to needle. With RS facing you, attach yarn. Beg with knit row, work in St st until armhole opening measures same as back, ending with WS row.

Next row: K20 (20, 21, 22, 23), place on holder to be used later for neckband. Using 3-needle BO, join rem 24 (28, 31, 34, 37) sts to corresponding back shoulder sts.

SLEEVES

Beg at cuff and with dpns, CO 52 (56, 56, 60, 64) sts. Join, being careful not to twist, pm to denote beg of rnd.

Rnds 1 and 3: Knit.

Rnds 2 and 4: Purl.

Beg working in St st (knit every round) until sleeve measures 3" from beg. Inc 1 st at beg and end of next rnd and every foll 6th rnd until there are 76 (80, 80, 84, 84) sts, switching to circular needle when ample sts to do so. Work even until total length of sleeve is 18 (18, 17½, 17½, 17)" or desired finished sleeve length, BO.

Recommended inc: M1 after first st and M1 before last st.

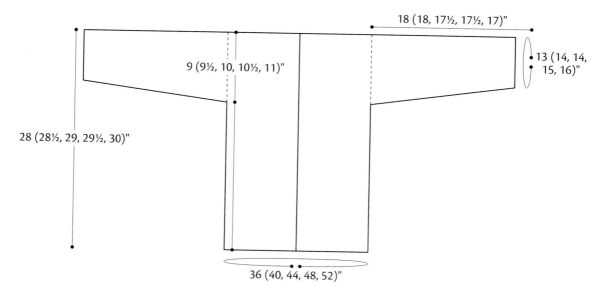

9 (9½, 10, 10½, 11)"

18 (18, 17½, 17½, 17)"

13 (14, 14, 15, 16)"

28 (28½, 29, 29½, 30)"

36 (40, 44, 48, 52)"

BACK NECKBAND

With RS facing you, return 20 (20, 21, 22, 23) sts from one front holder to needle. Work in St st for 3 (3, 3¼, 3½, 3¾)", ending with WS row. Return sts to holder. Rep with sts from other front holder. Use 3-needle BO to join these 2 sets of sts.

FINISHING

Sew back neckband to top of center back. Sew in sleeves. Weave in all ends.

CLASSIC RAGLAN **CARDIGAN**

Wide ribbing, pockets, and large buttons make this cardigan a real fashion classic. While basic in styling, the little extras make it a sweater that will be in your wardrobe for years to come.

Skill Level: Easy ◖■□□

Finished Bust Measurements: 38 (43, 48½, 54)"

Finished Length: 22 (23, 24¼, 25½)"

Sleeve Drop: 7½ (8, 9, 10)"

MATERIALS

Yarn: 11 (12, 14, 16) skeins of Kathmandu Aran from Queensland Collection (85% merino wool, 10% silk, 5% cashmere; 1¾ oz/50 g; 104 yds/95 m) in color 144, or approx 1100 (1250, 1450, 1650) yds of medium (worsted-weight) yarn ⬛4

Needles: Size 7 (4.5 mm) circular needles (16" and 29" long) or size needed to obtain gauge, size 7 double-pointed needles

Notions: Stitch holders; stitch markers; 5 buttons, approx 1½" diameter

Gauge: 18 sts and 28 rows = 4" in St st

POCKET LINING (MAKE 2)

CO 21 (21, 27, 27) sts. Work in St st (knit on RS, purl on WS) until piece measures 4 (4, 5, 5)", ending with WS row. Cut yarn and place sts on holder.

BODY

Beg at lower edge and with circular needle, CO 153 (177, 201, 225) sts.

Row 1 (RS): K3, *P3, K3, rep from * across row.

Row 2: P3, *K3, P3, rep from * across row.

Rep rows 1 and 2 until piece measures 3", ending with WS row.

Next row (RS): K36 (42, 48, 54) for right front, K81 (93, 105, 117) for back, K36 (42, 48, 54) for left front.

Beg with purl row (WS), work in St st until pieces measures 7 (7, 8, 8)" from beg, ending with WS row.

Attaching pocket linings: K10 (13, 15, 18), sl next 21 (21, 27, 27) sts to holder to be used later for pocket ribbing. With holder at front of work, K21 (21, 27, 27) of one pocket lining, K91 (109, 117, 135), sl next 21 (21, 27, 27) sts to 2nd holder to be used later for 2nd pocket ribbing. With holder at front of work, K21 (21, 27, 27) of 2nd pocket lining, K10 (13, 15, 18).

Work even in St st until piece measures 14 (15, 15½, 15½)" from beg, removing markers as you come to them and ending with RS row.

Dividing fronts and back:
Next row: P41 (47, 55, 63), place preceding 10 (10, 14, 18) sts on holder for underarm section, P81 (93, 105, 117), place preceding 10 (10, 14, 18) sts on 2nd holder for other underarm section, P31 (37, 41, 45). Leaving yarn attached, set aside body while knitting sleeves.

SLEEVES

Beg at cuff and with dpns, CO 48 (54, 54, 60) sts. Join, being careful not to twist, pm to denote beg of rnd.

All rnds: *K3, P3, rep from * around. Work in patt until cuff measures 3" from beg.

Change to St st and work even until total sleeve measures 5 (6, 6, 6)".

Cont working in St st while inc 1 st at beg and end of next rnd and every foll 6 (6, 4, 4) rnds until there are 68 (72, 82, 90) sts, switching to 16" circular needle when ample sts to do so.

Recommended inc: M1 after first st in rnd and M1 before last st in rnd.

Work even until total sleeve length is 18½ (19½, 20, 20)".

Cut yarn, leaving 18" tail (for seaming underarm sections tog).

Place 5 (5, 7, 9) sts from either side of beg-of-rnd marker on holder to be later seamed to body underarm sts. Place rem sts on spare needle or yarn strand, or divide on 2 holders.

JOINING SLEEVE AND BODY

With RS of body facing you, K31 (37, 41, 45) right front sts, pm, join 1 sleeve and K58 (62, 68, 72) sleeve sts, pm, K71 (83, 91, 99) back sts, pm, join 2nd sleeve and K58 (62, 68, 72) sleeve sts, pm, knit across rem 31 (37, 41, 45) left front sts—249 (281, 309. 333) total sts.

Purl 1 row.

RAGLAN YOKE DECREASING

Row 1 (RS): *Knit to 4 sts before marker, sl 1-K2tog-psso, K1, sm, K1, ssk, place this st back on LH needle, sl second st on LH needle over first stitch on LH needle, then sl LH needle st pw to RH needle, rep from * 3 more times, knit to end of row (16-st dec across row).

Rows 2 and 4: Purl.

Row 3: Knit.

Rows 5–32: Rep rows 1–4.

Row 33: Rep row 1.

Row 34: Purl.

Stitch counts:
Fronts: 15 (21, 25, 29) sts each.

Sleeves: 26 (30, 36, 40) sts each.

Back: 39 (51, 59, 67) sts.

Neck Shaping

Row 1 (RS): Ssk, *knit to 4 sts before marker, sl 1-K2tog-psso, K1, sm, K1, ssk, place this st back on LH needle, sl second st on LH needle over first stitch on LH needle, then sl LH needle st pw to RH needle, rep from * 3 more times, knit to last 2 sts, K2tog (18-st dec across row).

Rows 2 and 4: Purl.

Row 3: Ssk, knit even to last 2 sts, K2tog.

Work rows 1–4 a total of 3 (4, 5, 6) times. Cut yarn.

Stitch counts:
Fronts: 3 (5, 5, 5) sts each.

Sleeves: 14 (14, 16, 16) sts each.

Back: 27 (35, 39, 43) sts.

COLLAR

With RS facing you, PU 10 (13, 15, 19) sts along right front edge, K61 (73, 81, 85) from top of neck, PU 10 (13, 15, 19) sts along left front edge—81 (99, 111, 123) total sts.

Ribbing patt:
Row 1 (WS): K3, *P3, K3, rep from * across row.

Row 2: P3, *K3, P3, rep from * across row.

Rep rows 1 and 2 for patt.

Work in ribbing patt until collar measures 4 (4½, 4½, 5)", ending with RS row. BO in ribbing on WS.

BUTTON BAND

With RS of left front facing you, PU 117 (123, 129, 135) sts evenly along left front edge and collar edge.

Work in ribbing patt until band measures 2½", ending with RS row. BO in ribbing on WS.

BUTTONHOLE BAND

Work on right front same as button band until piece measures 1", ending with WS row. Work buttonholes as follows:

Row 1 (RS): Work in ribbing patt 6 (6, 8, 8) sts, BO 4 sts, *cont in ribbing patt 17 (18, 19, 20) sts, BO 4 sts, rep from * 3 more times, cont in ribbing patt 23 (25, 25, 27) sts.

Row 2: Work in ribbing patt 23 (25, 25, 27) sts, CO 4 sts, *cont in ribbing patt 17 (18, 19, 20) sts, CO 4 sts, rep from * 3 more times, cont in ribbing patt 6 (6, 8, 8) sts.

Work even in ribbing patt as estab until buttonhole band measures 2½", ending with RS row. BO in ribbing on WS.

POCKET RIBBINGS (MAKE 2)

With RS facing you, return one set of 21 (21, 27, 27) pocket-ribbing sts from holder to needle.

Rows 1, 3, and 5 (RS): K3, *P3, K3, rep from * across row.

Rows 2 and 4: P3, *K3, P3, rep from * across row.

BO in patt on WS. Rep for 2nd pocket.

FINISHING

Seam underarm sections tog using Kitchener st (page 77). Sew each side of pocket ribbing to front. Sew pocket linings to WS of front sections. Attach buttons to correspond with buttonholes. Weave in ends.

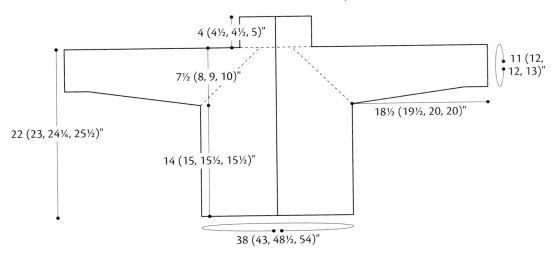

4 (4½, 4½, 5)"

7½ (8, 9, 10)"

11 (12, 12, 13)"

22 (23, 24¼, 25½)"

18½ (19½, 20, 20)"

14 (15, 15½, 15½)"

38 (43, 48½, 54)"

SIMPLY SUMMER TEE

Slightly flared in styling, this comfortable tee is perfect for carefree summer days. The textured border and simple-to-do keyhole closure add just the right fashion touches.

Skill Level: Intermediate ◼◼◼◻

Finished Bust Measurement: 36 (40½, 44¾, 49, 53½)"

Finished Length: 21½ (22, 22½, 23, 23½)"

Armhole Opening: 8½ (9, 9½, 10, 10½)"

MATERIALS

Yarn: 6 (7, 8, 9, 10) skeins of Savannah from Zitron (60% cotton, 20% linen, 20% rayon; 1.75 oz/50 g; 110 yds/90 m) in color 25, or approx 660 (740, 830, 940, 1050) yds of lightweight (DK) yarn (3)

Needles: Size 6 (4 mm) circular needles (16" and 29" long) or size required to attain gauge

Notions: Stitch markers; stitch holders; 1 button, approx ¾" diameter

Gauge: 22 sts and 28 rows = 4" in St st

BOTTOM BORDER

Beg at bottom and with 29" needle, CO 210 (234, 258, 282, 306) sts. Join, being careful not to twist, pm to denote beg of rnd. Work border patt as follows:

Rnds 1, 3, 5, 7, 9, and 11 (RS): Knit.

Rnds 2, 4, and 6: K2, P2, *K4, P2, rep from * to last 2 sts, K2.

Rnds 8, 10, and 12: P2, K2, *P4, K2, rep from * to last 2 sts, P2.

Rep rnds 1–12 once.

BODY

Beg working in St st, pm at 105 (117, 129, 141, 153) sts. Cont in St st until piece measures 12" from beg, working dec rnd at 4", 8", and 12"—198 (222, 246, 270, 294) sts after last dec.

Dec rnd: *K4, K2tog, knit to 6 sts before marker, ssk, K4, sm, rep from * once.

Armhole Borders

Armhole borders are knit in garter st, body in St st.

Rnds 1, 3, 5, 7, and 9: P6, K87 (99, 111, 123, 135), P6, sm, P6, K87 (99, 111, 123, 135), P6, sm.

Rnds 2, 4, 6, and 8: Knit.

Dividing Front and Back

K99 (111, 123, 135, 147), place sts on holder for front section.

Knit rem 99 (111, 123, 135, 147) sts. You will work back and forth on these sts for back section.

BACK

Keeping first and last 6 sts in garter st for armhole borders, work back section in St st and AT SAME TIME inc 1 st at armhole borders every 4th row a total of 10 times—119 (131, 143, 155, 167) total sts.

Recommended inc: For a nice smooth increase that is virtually invisible, work M1 using bar between border and body sts.

Cont in patt until piece measures 8½ (9, 9½, 10, 10½)" from dividing row, ending with WS row.

Arrange sts on 3 holders as follows:
First and third holders: 40 (46, 51, 55, 61) sts each.

Second holder: 39 (39, 41, 45, 45) sts.

FRONT

Return 99 (111, 123, 135, 147) front sts to needle. With WS facing you, attach yarn. Keeping first and last 6 sts in garter st for armhole borders, work front in St st and AT SAME TIME inc 1 st at armhole borders every 4th row a total of 10 times.

Knit in estab patt until front measures 1" from beg of armhole, placing markers on either side of 13 center sts and ending with RS row.

Front Border and Keyhole

Working in estab patt and cont armhole inc, AT SAME TIME beg center front border and keyhole as follows:

Rows 1, 3, 5, 7, and 9 (WS): K6, purl to marker, sm, K13, sm, purl to last 6 sts, K6.

Rows 2, 4, 6, 8, and 10: Knit.

Row 11: K6, purl to marker, sm, K6, BO 1 st, K6, sm, purl to last 6 sts, K6.

Row 12: Knit to bound-off stitch, attach 2nd skein of yarn, knit to end of row.

Working both sides at same time and using separate skeins of yarn, cont working front in St st, making armhole inc and working 6-st borders at armhole and center front as estab, until armhole opening measures 5", ending with WS row.

Left Side Neck Shaping

Work in patt across left front. Place rem sts on holder to be used later for right front. Turn work.

Next row: BO 10 sts, work in patt across rem sts.

Cont in patt as estab and AT SAME TIME dec 1 st at neck edge every other RS row a total of 9 (9, 10, 12, 12) times.

Recommended dec: Work to last 3 sts, ssk, K1.

Work even on rem 40 (46, 51, 55, 61) sts until front measures same as back to top of armhole. Join to corresponding back shoulder sts using 3-needle BO (page 76).

Right Side Neck Shaping

Place right front sts on needle and with RS facing, attach yarn.

Next row: BO 10 sts, work in patt across row.

Cont in patt as estab and AT SAME TIME dec 1 st at neck edge every other RS row a total of 9 (9, 10, 12, 12) times.

Recommended dec: K1, K2tog, work in patt to end of row.

Work even on rem 40 (46, 51, 55, 61) sts until front measures same as back to top of armhole. Join to corresponding back shoulder sts using 3-needle BO.

NECKBAND

With RS facing you, PU 30 sts along right side of front neck, K39 (39, 41, 45, 45) from back holder, PU 30 sts along left side of front neck—99 (99, 101, 105, 105) total sts.

Knit 4 rows. BO in knit on WS.

FINISHING

Weave in loose ends. Bring front neck edges together and secure with a button. Block if necessary.

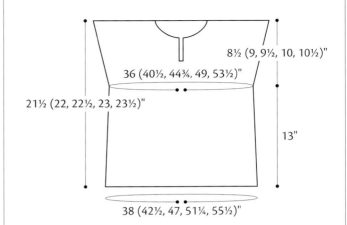

8½ (9, 9½, 10, 10½)"

36 (40½, 44¾, 49, 53½)"

21½ (22, 22½, 23, 23½)"

13"

38 (42½, 47, 51¼, 55½)"

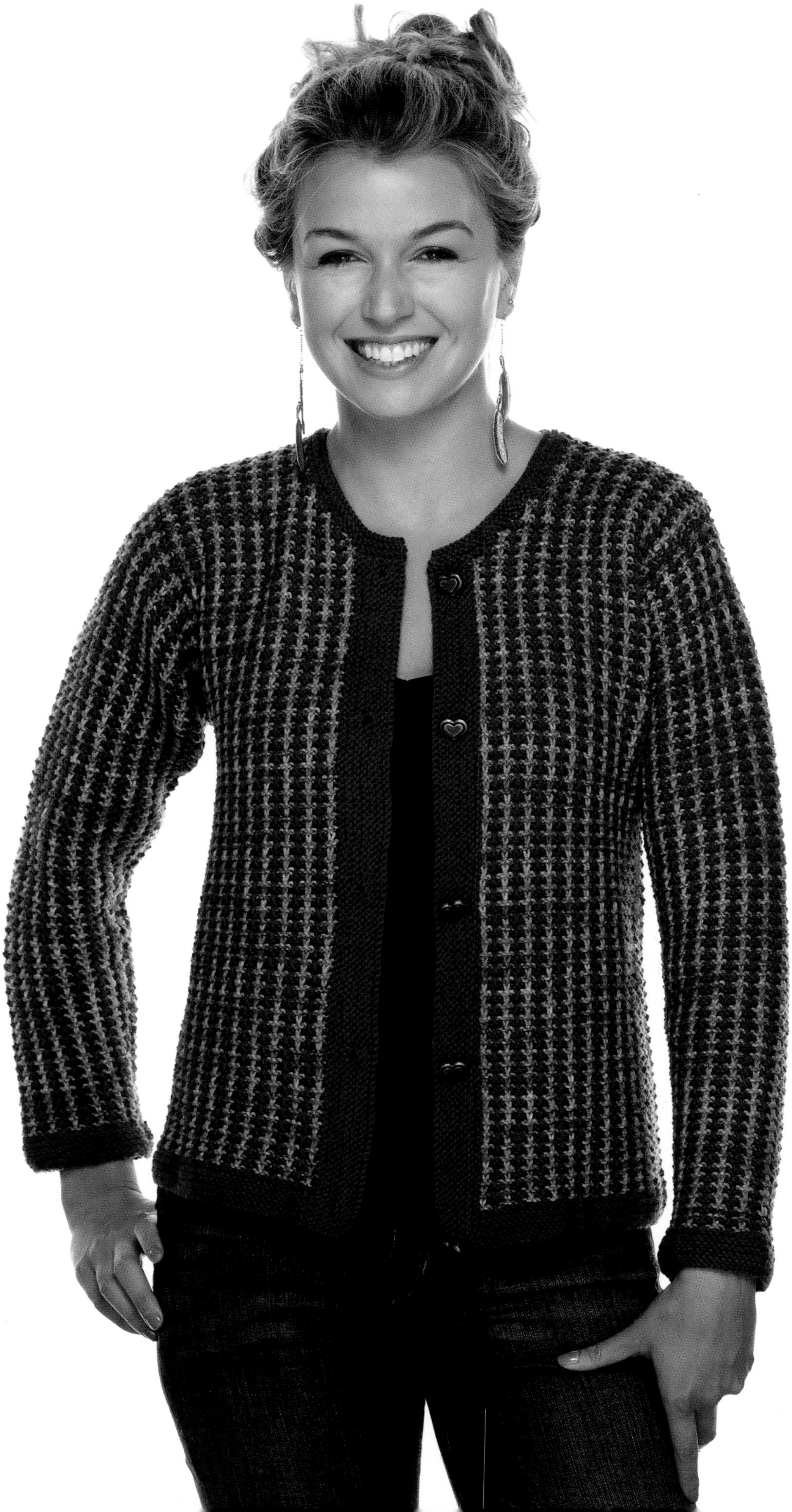

SLIP-STITCH TWEED JACKET

Slip-stitch patterns look complex, but because you work with only one color each row, they're quick and easy! For best results, pick a solid color that coordinates with the hand-painted yarn but isn't actually a color contained in that yarn. That way, the solid color won't become lost in places.

Skill Level: Easy ◖■□▷

Finished Bust Measurement: 34 (38, 42, 46, 50, 54)"

Finished Length: 23 (24, 24, 25, 25, 26)"

Sleeve Drop: 9 (9½, 9½, 10, 10, 11)"

MATERIALS

Yarn

MC: 6 (7, 8, 9, 10, 11) skeins of Gems from Louet (100% merino wool; 3.5 oz/100 g; 225 yds/203 m) in color 80, or approx 1300 (1450, 1650, 1875, 2125, 2400) yards of lightweight (DK) yarn **③**

CC: 5 (6, 7, 8, 9, 10) skeins of Sport Weight Claudia Hand Painted Yarn from Claudia and Co. (100% merino wool; 3.5 oz/100 g; 225 yds/203 m) in color Terra Cotta Blue, or approx 1100 (1250, 1450, 1675, 1925, 2200) yds of lightweight (DK) yarn **②**

Needles: Size 6 (4 mm) needles or size required to attain gauge, size 4 (3.5 mm) needles, size 4 circular needle (24" long)

Notions: Stitch markers; stitch holders; 5 buttons, ¾" diameter

Gauge: 24 sts and 44 rows = 4" in patt st

SLIP-STITCH PATTERN
(multiple of 4 + 3)

Sl all sts pw.

Row 1 (RS): With CC, K3, *sl 1 wyib, K3, rep from *.

Row 2: With CC, K3, *sl 1 wyif, K3, rep from * across row.

Row 3: With MC, K1, *sl 1 wyib, K3, rep from * to last 2 sts, sl 1 wyib, K1.

Row 4: With MC, K1, *sl 1 wyif, K3, rep from * to last 2 sts, sl 1 wyif, K1.

Rep rows 1–4 for patt.

BACK

Beg at lower edge and with size 4 needles and MC, CO 103 (115, 127, 139, 151, 163) sts. Work 10 rows in garter st. Change to size 6 needles and beg working in sl-st patt. Work even in patt until piece measures 14 (14½, 14½, 15, 15, 15)" from beg, ending with WS row.

Armhole Shaping

BO 8 (12, 16, 16, 20, 20) sts at beg of next 2 rows, working in patt to end of rows. Work even in patt on rem 87 (91, 95, 107, 111, 123) sts until armhole measures 9 (9½, 9½, 10, 10, 11)", ending with WS row. Divide sts on 3 holders as follows:

First and third holders: 29 (31, 31, 33, 35, 39) each.

Second holder: 29 (29, 33, 41, 41, 45) sts.

LEFT FRONT

Beg at lower edge with MC and size 4 needles, CO 47 (55, 63, 71, 79, 87) sts. Work as for back until piece measures 14 (14½, 14½, 15, 15, 15)" from beg, ending with WS row.

Armhole Shaping

Next row (RS): BO 8 (12, 16, 16, 20, 20) sts at beg of row, work in patt to end.

Work even in patt on rem 39 (43, 47, 55, 59, 67) sts until armhole measures 5 (5½, 5½, 5, 5, 6)", ending with WS row.

Neck Shaping

Cont in estab patt while dec 1 st at neck edge every RS row until 29 (31, 31, 33, 35, 39) sts rem.

Recommended dec: Knit to last 2 sts, K2tog.

Work even until left front measures same as back, ending with WS row. Join to corresponding back shoulder sts using 3-needle BO (page 76).

RIGHT FRONT

Work as for left front until piece measures 14 (14½, 14½, 15, 15, 15)" from beg, ending with RS row.

Armhole Shaping

Next row (WS): BO 8 (12, 16, 16, 20, 20) sts at beg of row, work in patt to end. Work even in patt until armhole measures 5 (5½, 5½, 5, 5, 6)", ending with WS row.

Neck Shaping

Cont in estab patt while dec 1 st at neck edge every RS row until 29 (31, 31, 33, 35, 39) sts rem.

Recommended dec: Ssk, work in patt to end of row.

Work even until right front measures same as back, ending with WS row. Join to corresponding back shoulder sts using 3-needle BO.

SLEEVES

Beg at lower edge and with size 4 needles and MC, CO 55 (59, 63, 63, 67, 71) sts.

Work in garter st for 10 rows. Change to size 6 needles and work 18 rows in sl-st patt, ending with WS row.

Inc 1 st at each end on next row and every foll 8th row until there are 87 (95, 95, 103, 103, 111) sts, then inc 1 st at each end of every 6th row until there are 107 (115, 115, 123, 123, 131) total sts, working new sts in sl-st patt.

Recommended inc: Lifted inc (L1) (page 74).

Work even until sleeve measures 20" or desired finished length, ending with WS row. BO.

BUTTON BAND

With RS facing you, size 4 needles, and MC, PU 108 (114, 114, 120, 120, 126) sts evenly along left front edge. Knit 12 rows, ending with RS row. BO firmly on WS.

BUTTONHOLE BAND

With RS facing you, size 4 needles, and MC, PU 108 (114, 114, 120, 120, 126) sts evenly along right front edge.

Rows 1–5: Knit.

Row 6 (RS): K5 (4, 4, 5, 5, 4), BO 3 sts, *K21 (23, 23, 24, 24, 26), BO 3 sts, rep from * to last 4 (3, 3, 4, 4, 3) sts, K4 (3, 3, 4, 4, 3).

Row 7: K4 (3, 3, 4, 4, 3), CO 3 sts, *K21 (23, 23, 24, 24, 26), CO 3 sts, rep from * to last 5 (4, 4, 5, 5, 4) sts, K5 (4, 4, 5, 5, 4).

Rows 8–12: Knit.

BO firmly on WS.

NECKBAND

With RS facing you, size 4 circular needle, and MC, PU 101 (101, 113, 121, 121, 125) sts around neck as follows:

> PU 36 (36, 40, 40, 40, 40) sts along right front neck edge.
>
> Knit 29 (29, 33, 41, 41, 45) from center back st holder.
>
> PU 36 (36, 40, 40, 40, 40) sts along left front neck edge.

Rows 1–4: Knit.

BO on WS.

FINISHING

Sew sleeves to body, then sew side and sleeve seams using the flat seam assembly technique (page 76).

Weave in loose ends. Sew buttons on button band to correspond to buttonholes. Block.

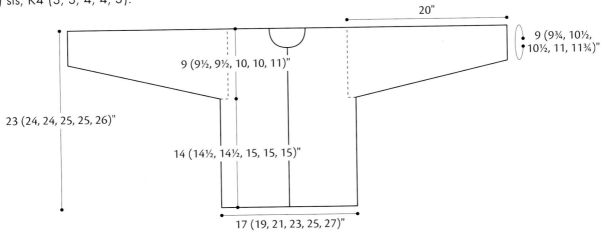

20"

9 (9¾, 10½, 10½, 11, 11¾)"

9 (9½, 9½, 10, 10, 11)"

23 (24, 24, 25, 25, 26)"

14 (14½, 14½, 15, 15, 15)"

17 (19, 21, 23, 25, 27)"

LAZY DAYS TEE

Be ready for those relaxing, warm sunny days with this easy-to-knit top. Its basic yet classy styling makes it great for casual as well as evening wear. You'll want to make several!

Skill Level: Easy ◀■□▷

Finished Bust Measurement: 36 (40, 44, 48, 52)"

Finished Length: 20 (21, 22, 23, 24)"

Sleeve Depth: 8 (8½, 8½, 9, 9½)"

MATERIALS

Yarn: 6 (7, 8, 9, 10) skeins of Cotton Rich DK by Cascade Yarns (64% cotton, 36% polyamide; 1¾ oz/50 g; 135 yds/118 m) in color 6335, or approx 810 (980, 1180, 1325, 1500) yds of lightweight (DK) yarn ⬤③

Needles: Size 5 (3.75 mm) circular needles (16" and 29" long) or size required to attain gauge

Notions: Stitch markers, stitch holders

Gauge: 20 sts and 32 rows = 4" in patt st

PATTERN STITCH
(multiple of 5 + 5)

In the Round:

Rnd 1: K1, P3, *K2, P3, rep from * to last st, K1.

Rnd 2: Knit.

Rep rnds 1 and 2 for patt when working in the round.

Back and Forth:

Row 1 (RS): K1, P3, *K2, P3, rep from * to last st, K1.

Row 2: Purl.

Rep rows 1 and 2 for patt when working back and forth.

BODY

Beg at bottom edge and with 29" circular needle, CO 180 (200, 220, 240, 260) sts. Join, being careful not to twist, pm to denote beg of round. Work in patt st until piece measures 12 (12½, 13½, 14, 14½)" from beg or desired length to armhole, ending with rnd 1.

Dividing Front and Back

Work in estab patt 96 (107, 118, 131, 142) sts, place last 12 (14, 16, 22, 24) sts worked on holder to be used later for underarm, cont in estab patt to end of rnd. Cut yarn. Place last 6 (7, 8, 11, 12) sts of rnd and first 6 (7, 8, 11, 12) sts of rnd on 2nd st holder for 2nd underarm.

BACK

With RS facing you, attach yarn. Working back and forth and keeping patt st as estab, work even on 78 (86, 94, 98, 106) sts of back section until armhole measures 8 (8½, 8½, 9, 9½)", ending with WS row.

Divide sts on 3 st holders as follows:
First and third holders: 22 (25, 28, 29, 32) sts each.

Second holder: 34 (36, 38, 40, 42) sts.

FRONT

Work as for back until armhole section measures 4 (4½, 4½, 5, 5½)", ending with WS row.

Neck Shaping

Work 22 (25, 28, 29, 32) sts in patt, attach 2nd skein of yarn, and work in patt next 34 (36, 38, 40, 42) sts. Place these sts on holder to be used later for front neck, work in patt rem 22 (25, 28, 29, 32) sts.

Working both sides at same time, cont even in patt on rem sts until front measures same as back, ending with WS row. Use 3-needle BO (page 76) to join front and back shoulder sts.

NECKBAND

With RS facing you and with 16" circular needle, sl 34 (36, 38, 40, 42) sts from back holder to needle, attach yarn and PU 22 sts along left front neck edge, K34 (36, 38, 40, 42) from front holder, PU 22 sts along right front neck edge. Pm to denote beg of rnd—112 (116, 120, 124, 128) sts.

Rnd 1: Purl.

Rnd 2: K54 (56, 58, 60, 62), K2tog, K33 (35, 37, 39, 41), K2tog, K21 (21, 21, 21, 21).

BO firmly in purl.

SLEEVES

With RS facing you and with 16" circular needle, beg underarm sts as follows: sl first 6 (7, 8, 11, 12) sts from holder to needle, pm to denote beg of rnd, attach yarn and knit rem 6 (7, 8, 11, 12) sts from holder. These 12 (14, 16, 22, 24) sts will be referred to as gusset sts. PU 88 (93, 93, 98, 103) sts around armhole opening, knit across rem 6 (7, 8, 11, 12) gusset sts. You should be back at marker indicating beg of rnd—100 (107, 109, 120, 127) total sts.

Underarm Shaping

Rnd 1: K4 (5, 6, 9, 10) gusset sts, K2tog, P3, *K2, P3, rep from * to last 6 (7, 8, 11, 12) gusset sts, ssk, K4 (5, 6, 9, 10)—98 (105, 107, 118, 125) sts.

Rnd 2 and all even-numbered rnds: Purl gusset sts on each side of marker, knit rem sts.

Rnd 3: K3 (4, 5, 8, 9) gusset sts, K2tog, P3, *K2, P3, rep from * to last 5 (6, 7, 10, 11) gusset sts, ssk, K3 (4, 5, 8, 9)—96 (103, 105, 116, 123) sts.

Cont underarm gusset dec as estab, having 1 less gusset st before first dec and 1 less gusset st after last dec until 90 (95, 95, 100, 105) sts rem, ending with even-numbered rnd.

Body of Sleeve

Rnd 1: K1, P3, *K2, P3, rep from * to last st, K1.

Rnd 2: Knit.

Rep these 2 rnds until sleeve measures 3 (3½, 4, 4½, 5)" from armhole edge or desired finished length, ending with rnd 2. BO in patt.

FINISHING

Weave in all ends.

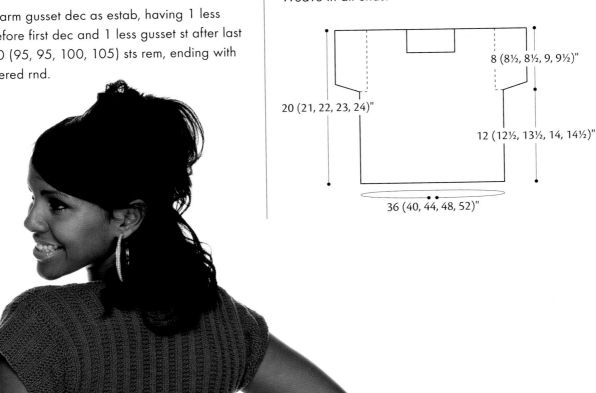

20 (21, 22, 23, 24)"

8 (8½, 8½, 9, 9½)"

12 (12½, 13½, 14, 14½)"

36 (40, 44, 48, 52)"

EASY STRIPED **PULLOVER**

Knit in just two pieces from side to side, this sweater uses a variegated yarn with fairly long color runs to create the striping. You'll knit two rows from one skein of yarn, and then two rows from a second skein of the same colorway of yarn, making sure that the starting point is at a different color for each skein. Because you work only two rows at a time from each skein, you can simply carry the yarn that's not being used up the side. Thus, you won't have a lot of tails to weave in when the sweater is finished.

Skill Level: Easy ◖■□▷

Finished Bust Measurement: 36 (40, 44, 48, 52)"

Finished Length: 24 (24½, 25, 25¼, 25¼)"

Sleeve Drop: 9 (9½, 10, 10¼, 10¼)"

MATERIALS

Yarn: 10 (12, 13, 15, 17) skeins of Kureyon by Noro (100% wool; 3.5 oz/100 g; 110 yds/100 m) in color 207, or approx 1100 (1240, 1400, 1580, 1780) yds of variegated medium (worsted-weight) yarn (4)

Needles: Size 7 (4.5 mm) circular needles (16" and 40" or longer) or size needed to attain gauge

Notions: Size G (4 mm) crochet hook (for provisional CO); stitch markers; stitch holders; smooth-textured scrap of worsted-weight yarn; 3 buttons, ¾" diameter

Gauge: 18 sts and 24 rows = 4" in St std

STRIPED PATTERN

Work two rows from one skein of variegated yarn, and then two rows from the second skein of the same yarn, making sure the starting point on the second skein is at a different color than the first skein. Alternate skeins every two rows to create the striped pattern. Don't cut the yarn when switching skeins; simply carry the unused strand up the side edge.

LEFT SLEEVE

Beg at cuff and with shorter needle, CO 40 (46, 52, 52, 58) sts. Work cuff as follows:

Rows 1–4: Knit. Mark row 1 as RS.

Rows 5, 7, and 9: P4, *K2, P4, rep from * across row.

Rows 6, 8, and 10: Purl.

Beg working in St st (knit RS rows, purl WS rows), inc 1 st at beg and end of next row and every foll 6th row until there are 82 (86, 90, 94, 98) sts. Work even until total sleeve length is 20" or desired length, ending with RS row. Do not BO. Cut yarn, leaving 1½ yd tail; set sleeve aside.

Recommended inc: M1 after first st. Work to 1 st before end, M1.

RIGHT SLEEVE

Work same as left sleeve *except* work 1 additional row to end with WS row.

Do not BO. Cut yarn.

FRONT AND BACK

With longer needle, scrap yarn, and a new working strand, provisionally CO 68 sts for right edge of front (page 73). With RS facing you, K82 (86, 90, 94, 98) right sleeve sts on same needle as CO sts, then provisionally CO 68 sts for right edge of back—218 (222, 226, 230, 234) total sts.

Work in St st until piece measures 4½ (5½, 6½, 7½, 8½)" from provisional CO edges, ending with a RS row.

Dividing Front and Back

P104 (106, 108, 110, 112) sts for back, place next 10 sts on holder to be used later for neckband, place rem 104 (106, 108, 110, 112) sts on 2nd holder to be used later for front.

BACK

Cont in St st on 104 (106, 108, 110, 112) back sts, dec 1 st at neck edge on next 5 RS rows—99 (101, 103, 105, 107) sts.

Recommended dec: K2tog, knit to end of row.

Work even 55 additional rows, ending with RS row. Inc 1 st at neck edge on next 5 rows—104 (106, 108, 110, 112) sts.

Recommended inc: K1, M1, knit to end of row.

Place back sts on holder.

FRONT

With WS facing you, return 104 (106, 108, 110, 112) front sts to working needle. Purl 1 row. Working in St st, dec 1 st at neck edge every row for a total of 20 times, ending with WS row. Work even on rem 84 (86, 88, 90, 92) sts for 6 rows.

Recommended dec: On RS rows, knit to last 3 sts, ssk, K1. On WS rows, P1, P2tog tb1, purl to end of row.

Front Opening

Row 1 (RS): Knit until 20 sts rem, place these sts on holder to be used later for button band.

Row 2: Purl.

Row 3: Knit to end of row. Provisionally CO 20 sts.

Row 4: Purl.

Work even in St st for 6 rows.

Inc 1 st at neck edge every row a total of 20 times, ending with WS row—104 (106, 108, 110, 112) sts.

JOINING FRONT AND BACK

Knit across front sts, provisionally CO 10 sts, knit across back sts (from holder).

Cont working in St st for 4½ (5½, 6½, 7½, 8½)" from neck edge, ending with WS row.

JOINING LEFT SLEEVE TO BODY OF SWEATER

Place first 68 and last 68 sts on separate needles. Using Kitchener st (page 77), graft left sleeve to rem sts. BO left front and back sts tog using 3-needle BO (page 76). Remove provisional CO from right edge of front and back sections, place sts on needles, and join front and back tog using 3-needle BO.

BUTTON BAND

Remove provisional CO from center front opening and place these 20 sts on needle with RS facing you. Work 8 rows in garter st. BO kw on WS.

BUTTONHOLE BAND

With WS facing you, return 20 sts from center front holder to needle.

Rows 1 (RS)–4: Knit.

Row 5: K4, BO 2 sts, K6, BO 2 sts, K6.

Row 6: K6, CO 2 sts, K6, CO 2 sts, K4.

Rows 7–9: Knit.

BO on WS. Sew bottom of button band to sweater body. Lap buttonhole band over button band and sew down at bottom of band. Attach buttons to correspond with buttonholes.

NECKBAND

With RS facing you and longer circular needle, PU 6 sts along top of buttonhole band, 24 (24, 26, 26, 28) sts along right front edge, pm, K10 from holder, pm, PU 54 (54, 58, 58, 62) sts across back, pm, remove provisional CO, place sts on needle, and knit those 10 sts, pm, PU 24 (24, 26, 26, 28) sts along left front edge, PU 6 sts along top of button band—134 (134, 142, 142, 150) total sts.

Rows 1, 3, and 7 (WS): Knit.

Row 2: *Knit to 2 sts before marker, K2tog, sm, K10, sm, K2tog, rep from * once, knit to end of row.

Row 4: K3, BO 2 sts for buttonhole, *knit to 2 sts before marker, K2tog, sm, K10, sm, K2tog, rep from * once, knit to end of row.

Row 5: Knit until 3 sts rem on left needle, CO 2 sts, K3.

Rows 6 and 8: Rep row 2.

BO on WS. Weave in loose ends.

FINISHING

Sew underarm and side seams. Sew on buttons to correspond to buttonholes. Weave in any loose ends.

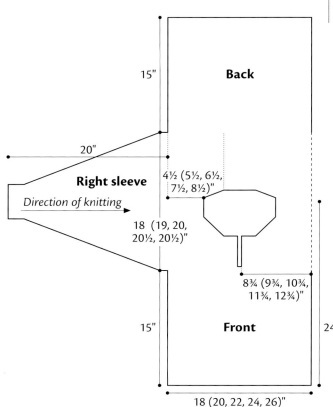

15"

Back

20"

Right sleeve

Direction of knitting

4½ (5½, 6½, 7½, 8½)"

18 (19, 20, 20½, 20½)"

8¾ (9¾, 10¾, 11¾, 12¾)"

15"

Front

18 (20, 22, 24, 26)"

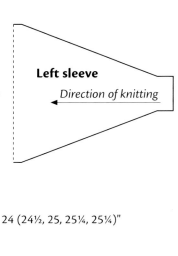

Left sleeve

Direction of knitting

24 (24½, 25, 25¼, 25¼)"

CABLED IN COMFORT

Cabled borders add texture to this otherwise basic cardigan. Its short sleeves make it perfect when just a little extra warmth is desired. Quick to knit, this sweater is worked in pieces from the bottom up. Then the pieces are joined to finish the raglan-yoke shaping.

Skill Level: Intermediate ◼◼◼◻

Finished Bust Measurement:	36 (39½, 44, 48½, 52)"
Finished Length:	26 (26, 27, 27, 28)"
Sleeve Drop:	9 (9, 10, 10, 11)"

MATERIALS

Yarn: 14 (16, 18, 21, 23) skeins of Sulka from Mirasol (60% wool, 20% alpaca, 20% silk; 1¾ oz/50 g; 55 yds/50 m) in color 207, or approx 770 (870, 980, 1110, 1260) yds of bulky-weight yarn ⑤

Needles: Size 10 (6 mm) straight and circular needles (24" and 36" or longer) or size required to attain gauge, size 9 (5.5 mm) straight and/or circular needles (24" long)

Notions: Stitch markers; stitch holders; cable needle; 2 buttons, approx 1¼" diameter

Gauge: 14 sts and 18 rows = 4" in St st

BACK

With size 9 needles, CO 73 (79, 87, 95, 101) sts.

Knit 12 rows, marking row 1 as RS of work. Switch to size 10 needles and work in St st, dec 1 st at each end of RS row when work measures 3", 6", 9", 12", and 15". Work even on rem 63 (69, 77, 85, 91) sts until piece measures 17" from beg, ending with WS row.

Cont in St st, BO 3 (5, 6, 7, 8) sts at beg of next 2 rows—57 (59, 65, 71, 75) sts rem. Cut yarn and place sts on holder.

LEFT FRONT

Left Front Border Pattern (17 sts)

Rows 1, 3, and 7 (RS): K3, P1, K4, P1, K4, P1, K3.

Rows 2, 4, 6, and 8: K4, P4, K1, P4, K1.

Row 5: K3, P1, 2/2CB, P1, 2/2CB, P1, K3.

Rep rows 1–8 for patt.

2/2CB: Sl next 2 sts to cn and hold in back, K2, K2 from cn.

With size 9 needles, CO 45 (48, 52, 56, 59) sts.

Row 1 (RS): Knit to last 17 sts, work row 1 of left front border patt.

Row 2: Work row 2 of left front border patt over first 17 sts, knit to end of row.

Work 10 more rows, cont in left front border patt as estab and garter st over rem sts.

Switch to size 10 needles and work in St st, maintaining left front border patt and dec 1 st at side edge on RS row when work measures 3", 6", 9", 12", and 15" from beg. Work even on rem 40 (43, 47, 51, 54) sts until piece measures 17" from beg, ending with WS row.

Recommended dec: K1, ssk, work to end of row.

BO 3 (5, 6, 7, 8) sts. Cut yarn. Place rem 37 (38, 41, 44, 46) sts on holder.

RIGHT FRONT

Right Front Border Pattern (17 sts)

Rows 1, 3, and 7 (RS): K3, P1, K4, P1, K4, P1, K3.

Rows 2, 4, 6, and 8: K4, P4, K1, P4, K4.

Row 5: K3, P1, 2/2CF, P1, 2/2CF, P1, K3.

Rep rows 1–8 for patt.

2/2CF: Sl next 2 sts to cn and hold in front, K2, K2 from cn.

With size 9 needles, CO 45 (48, 52, 56, 59) sts.

Row 1 (RS): Work row 1 of right front border patt over first 17 sts, knit to end of row.

Row 2: Knit to last 17 sts, work row 2 of right front border patt over last 17 sts.

Work 10 more rows, maintaining right front border patt as estab and garter st over rem sts.

Switch to size 10 needles and work in St st, maintaining right front border patt and dec 1 st at side edge on RS row when work measures 3", 6", 9", 12", and 15" from beg. Work even on rem 40 (43, 47, 51, 54) sts until piece measures 17" from beg, ending with RS row.

Recommended dec: Work to last 3 sts, K2tog, K1.

BO 3 (5, 6, 7, 8) sts, purl to end of row. Cut yarn. Place rem 37 (38, 41, 44, 46) sts on holder.

SLEEVES

With size 9 needles, CO 62 (68, 74, 82, 86) sts. Knit 12 rows, marking row 1 as RS.

Change to size 10 needles and work even in St st until sleeve measures 2½" from beg, ending with WS row.

Cont in St st, BO 3 (5, 6, 7, 8) sts at beg of next 2 rows for underarm. Cut yarn and place rem 56 (58, 62, 68, 70) sts on holder.

RAGLAN YOKE

With RS facing you and maintaining patt as estab, use longer size 10 circular needle to work across 37 (38, 41, 44, 46) right front sts, pm, work across 56 (58, 62, 68, 70) sleeve sts, pm, work across 57 (59, 65, 71, 75) back sts, pm, work across 56 (58, 62, 68, 70) sleeve sts, pm, work across 37 (38, 41, 44, 46) left front sts—243 (251, 271, 295, 307) total sts. Purl 1 row even.

Maintaining border patts as estab, work yoke shaping as follows:

Row 1 (RS): *Work to 3 sts before marker, ssk, K1, sm, K1, K2tog; rep from * 3 times, work to end of row (8-st dec).

Row 2: Purl.

Work rows 1 and 2 a total of 11 (12, 13, 15, 15) times, ending with WS row—155 (155, 167, 175, 187) sts.

NECKBAND

Switch to smaller needles and work neckband as follows:

Rows 1 and 3 (RS): *Knit to 3 sts before marker, K2tog, K1, sm, K1, K2tog, rep from * 3 times, knit to end of row.

Rows 2 and 4: Knit.

Work buttonholes over rows 5–12 as follows:

Row 5: K5, attach separate piece of yarn (approx 1 yd long) and knit next 7 sts, attach 2nd skein of yarn and knit rem sts, maintaining decs as estab.

Rows 6–11: Knit, working each "set" of sts from separate yarns and maintaining decs as estab.

Row 12: Knit, working all sts from same skein of yarn, completing buttonholes. Other yarns may now be cut.

Rows 13–17: Purl, maintaining decs as estab.

BO kw on WS.

FINISHING

Sew side seams, sleeve seams, and underarm seams. Sew on buttons to correspond to buttonholes. Weave in loose ends. Block.

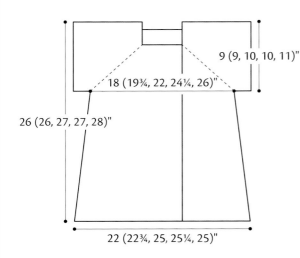

9 (9, 10, 10, 11)"

18 (19¾, 22, 24¼, 26)"

26 (26, 27, 27, 28)"

22 (22¾, 25, 25¼, 25)"

Left Front Border

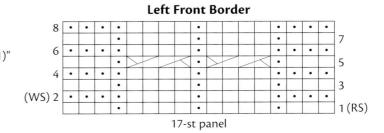

17-st panel

Right Front Border

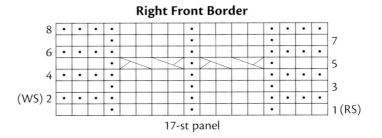

17-st panel

Key

☐ K on RS, P on WS

▫ P on RS, K on WS

⬜ 2/2CF: sl 2 sts to cn and hold in front, K2, K2 from cn

⬜ 2/2CB: sl 2 sts to cn and hold in back, K2, K2 from cn

BUTTON-UP COVER-UP

This cover-up is a combination of a cape, poncho, and shawl. But, whatever you choose to call it, it's sure to become a wardrobe favorite. Whether done in a beautiful hand-painted yarn as shown or in a solid color to showcase gorgeous buttons, you'll be the envy of all around. Because of the loose styling, the finished bust measurement isn't crucial—simply pick the set of numbers closest to the finished bust measurement you would normally make and go for it! I've even given you two options for finished length.

Skill Level: Easy ◖■□▷	
Finished Bust Measurement: 36–40 (42–46, 48–52)"	
Finished Length	
Shorter Version: 24 (25, 26)"	
Longer Version: 28 (29, 30)"	

MATERIALS

Yarn: 6 (7, 8) skeins for shorter version, 7 (8, 9) skeins for longer version of Oregon Worsted Stripe by Interlacements (100% merino wool; 4 oz/113 g, 280 yds/255 m) in color 414, or 1680 (1960, 2240) yds for shorter version, 1960 (2240, 2520) for longer version of worsted-weight yarn 〔4〕

Needles: Size 7 (4.5 mm) circular needle (29" long) or size required to attain gauge, size 6 (4 mm) circular needle (24" long)

Notions: Stitch holders; stitch markers; 6 buttons, ¾" diameter

Gauge: 20 sts and 28 rows = 4" in St st on larger needle

CENTER BACK

Beg at bottom edge and with size 7 needle, CO 70 (80, 90) sts. Work in St st (knit on RS, purl on WS) until piece measures 22 (23, 24)" for shorter or 26 (27, 28)" for longer version, ending with WS row.

Neck shaping: On next RS row, K20 (25, 30), sl next 30 sts to holder, attach 2nd skein of yarn, and K20 (25, 30).

Working both sides at same time with separate skeins of yarn, work even in St st until piece measures 2" from beg of neck shaping, ending with WS row. Cut yarn. Place each set of sts on individual holders to be joined later to front shoulders.

RIGHT FRONT

Beg at bottom and with size 7 needle, CO 32 (37, 42) sts. Work in St st until piece measures 20 (21, 22)" from beg for shorter or 24 (25, 26)" for longer version, ending with RS row.

Neck shaping: On next WS row, purl to last 12 sts. Put these 12 sts on holder.

Work even on rem 20 (25, 30) sts until piece measures same as back. Join these shoulder sts to corresponding sts on center back section using 3-needle BO (page 76).

LEFT FRONT

Beg at bottom and with size 7 needle, CO 32 (37, 42) sts. Work in St st until piece measures 20 (21, 22)" from beg for shorter or 24 (25, 26)" for longer version, ending with WS row.

Neck shaping: On next RS row, knit to last 12 sts. Put these 12 sts on holder. Work even on rem 20 (25, 30) sts until piece measures same as back. Join these shoulder sts to corresponding sts on center back section using 3-needle BO.

SIDE PANELS (MAKE 2)

With RS facing you and size 6 circular needle, PU 240 (250, 260) sts for shorter or 280 (290, 300) sts for longer version along 1 side edge (across both front and back sections). Knit 9 rows in garter st, ending with WS row.

Switch to size 7 needle and cont in St st until side panel measures 2" from PU row, ending with WS row.

Beg dec as follows:
Row 1 (RS): K1, ssk, K113 (118, 123) for shorter or K133 (138, 143) for longer version, ssk, pm, K4, pm, K2tog, K113 (118, 123) for shorter or K133 (138, 143) for longer version, K2tog, K1.

Row 2: Purl.

Row 3: K1, ssk, knit to 2 sts before marker, ssk, sm, K4, sm, K2tog, knit to last 3 sts, K2tog, K1.

Row 4: Purl.

Rep rows 3 and 4 until 100 (102, 100) sts rem, ending with RS row.

Change to size 6 needle and work side-panel border as follows:

Rows 1, 3, 5, 7, 9, and 11 (WS): Knit.

Rows 2, 4, 6, 8, 10, and 12: K1f&b, knit to last 2 sts, K1f&b, K1.

BO on WS.

Work second side panel same as first panel.

BOTTOM BANDS

Left Front

With RS facing you and size 6 circular needle, PU 32 (37, 42) sts along CO edge of left front, PU 68 sts for shorter or 88 sts for longer version along side panel—100 (105, 110) total sts for shorter or 120 (125, 130) sts for longer version.

Rows 1, 3, 5, 7, 9, and 11 (WS): Knit.

Rows 2, 4, 6, 8, 10, and 12: Knit to last 2 sts, K1f&b, K1.

BO on WS.

Right Front

With RS facing you and size 6 circular needle, PU 68 sts for shorter or 88 sts for longer version along "sleeve" edge, PU 32 (37, 42) sts along CO edge of front section—100 (105, 110) total sts for shorter or 120 (125, 130) sts for longer version.

Rows 1, 3, 5, 7, 9, and 11 (WS): Knit.

Rows 2, 4, 6, 8, 10, and 12: K1f&b, knit to end of row.

BO on WS.

Back

With RS facing you and smaller circular needle, PU 68 sts for shorter or 88 sts for longer version along sleeve edge, PU 70 (80, 90) sts along CO edge of back, and PU 68 sts for shorter or 88 sts for longer version along second sleeve—206 (216, 226) total sts for shorter or 246 (256, 266) sts for longer version.

Rows 1, 3, 5, 7, 9, and 11 (WS): Knit.

Rows 2, 4, 6, 8, 10, and 12: K1f&b, knit to last 2 sts, K1f&b, K1.

BO on WS.

NECKBAND

With RS facing you and smaller circular needle, PU 114 sts as follows: K12 from right side front holder, pm, PU 30 sts along right side of neck edge, pm, K30 from back neck holder, pm, PU 30 sts along left side of neck edge, pm, K12 from left side front holder.

Rows 1, 3, 5, 7, 9, and 11 (WS): Knit.

Rows 2, 4, 6, 8, 10, and 12: *Knit to 2 sts before marker, K2tog, sm, K2tog, rep from * 3 times, knit to end of row.

BO on WS.

LEFT BUTTON BAND

With RS facing you, PU 123 (128, 133) sts for shorter or 143 (148, 153) sts for longer version along left center front edge. Beg with WS, knit 12 rows. BO on WS.

RIGHT BUTTONHOLE BAND

With RS facing you, PU 123 (128, 133) sts for shorter or 143 (148, 153) sts for longer version along right center-front edge.

Rows 1–5: Knit.

Row 6 (RS): K3 for shorter or K23 for longer version, *BO 2 sts, K21 (22, 23), rep from * to last 5 sts, BO 2 sts, K3.

Row 7: K3, *CO 2 sts, K21 (22, 23), rep from * until 3 sts for shorter or 23 sts for longer version rem on left needle, CO 2 sts, K3 for shorter or K23 for longer version.

Rows 8–12: Knit.

BO on WS.

FINISHING

Sew angled edges of bottom bands and sleeve bands together. Sew buttons on left front band to correspond to buttonholes on right front band. Weave in ends.

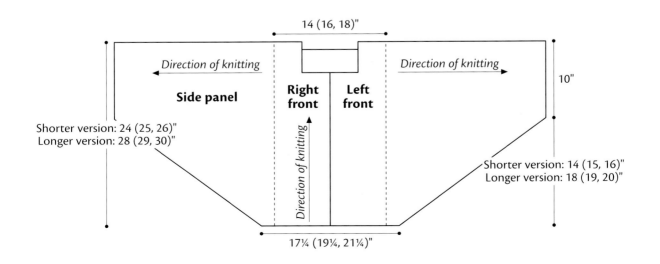

14 (16, 18)"

Direction of knitting   *Direction of knitting*

Side panel   **Right front**   **Left front**

10"

Shorter version: 24 (25, 26)"
Longer version: 28 (29, 30)"

Direction of knitting

Shorter version: 14 (15, 16)"
Longer version: 18 (19, 20)"

17¼ (19¼, 21¼)"

DIAGONAL YOKE JACKET

The diagonal garter-stitch yoke on this jacket adds extra flair and style, making this otherwise basic jacket very classic looking. Dress it up or dress it down—it's sure to become a wardrobe favorite that can easily go from day to nighttime wear!

Skill Level: Easy ◖■☐☐

Finished Bust Measurement: 36 (40, 44, 48, 52)"

Finished Length: Approx 26 (26, 27, 27½, 28)"

Sleeve Drop: 9 (9, 9½, 10, 10½)"

MATERIALS

Yarn: 2 (3, 3, 3, 4) skeins of Wool Twist by Happy Hands Yarn (100% merino wool; 8 oz /226 g; 560 yds/80 m) in color Here Comes the Sun, or approx 1050 (1175, 1340, 1525, 1750) yds of a medium (worsted-weight) yarn ❨4❩

Needles: Size 8 (5 mm) needles or size required to attain gauge, size 8 circular needle (24" or longer), size 8 double-pointed needles

Notions: Stitch markers; stitch holders; locking-type stitch marker; 2 buttons, approx 1" diameter

Gauge: 16 sts and 32 rows = 4" in garter st

YOKE

Making Triangles

With straight needles, CO 1 st.

Row 1: K1f&b—2 sts.

Row 2: K1f&b in first st, K1—3 sts.

Row 3: K1f&b in first st, K1f&b in second st, K1—5 sts. Pm to denote this side as RS.

Row 4: Knit.

Row 5: K1f&b in first st, knit until 2 sts rem, K1f&b in next st, K1.

Rep rows 4 and 5 until 45 (49, 53, 57, 61) sts, ending with RS row.

Cut yarn and place sts on holder. Rep to make 3 more triangles. Leave last triangle on needle; do not cut yarn.

Joining Triangles

With circular needle, knit across last triangle, pm, CO 8 sts for shoulder, pm, knit across 2nd triangle, pm, knit across 3rd triangle, pm, CO 8 sts for shoulder, pm, knit across rem triangle—196 (212, 228, 244, 260) total sts.

Complete yoke as follows:
Row 1 (RS): K2tog, knit to 2 sts before marker, K2tog, sm, K8, sm, K2tog, knit to 2 sts before marker, K2tog, sm, K2tog, knit to 2 sts before marker, K2tog, sm, K8, sm, K2tog, knit to last 2 sts, K2tog—8 st dec.

Row 2: Knit.

Rep rows 1 and 2 until 100 sts rem, ending with RS row. BO kw on WS.

BODY

With RS of yoke facing you, PU sts along bottom of yoke as follows: PU 32 (34, 36, 38, 40) sts along left front yoke, pm, CO 8 (12, 16, 20, 24) sts for underarm, pm, PU 64 (68, 72, 76, 80) sts along back of yoke, pm, CO 8 (12, 16, 20, 24) sts for underarm, pm, PU 32 (34, 36, 38, 40) sts along right front yoke—144 (160, 176, 192, 208) total sts.

Note: Use knitted CO (page 73) to CO in middle of row.

Beg with WS row, work in St st until piece measures 16½ (16½, 17, 17, 17)" from armhole or approx ½" less than desired finished length, ending with WS row.

Knit 5 rows, ending with RS row. BO kw on WS.

SLEEVES

With RS facing you, beg at center of underarm section, PU 4 (6, 8, 10, 12) sts along underarm, pm, PU 72 (72, 76, 80, 84) sts around armhole opening, pm, PU 4 (6, 8, 10, 12) sts along underarm, pm of a different color to denote beg of rnd—80 (84, 92, 100, 108) sts.

Sleeve Gusset

Rnd 1: Knit.

Rnd 2: Knit to 2 sts before marker, K2tog, sm, knit to next marker, sm, ssk, knit to end of rnd.

Rep rnds 1 and 2 until just 1 st rem between markers. At this point all markers except beg-of-rnd marker may be removed—74 (74, 78, 82, 86) sts.

Sleeve Body

Cont in St st, dec 1 st at beg and end of every 6 (6, 5, 4, 3) rnds until 60 (66, 72, 76, 82) sts rem, then dec 1 st at beg and end of every 6 (5, 4, 4, 4) rnds until 44 (48, 50, 54, 56) sts rem. Work even until sleeve measures 20½" or approx ½" less than desired finished sleeve length, switching to dpns when too few sts for circular needle.

Sleeve Cuff

Rnds 1 and 3: Purl.

Rnds 2 and 4: Knit.

BO pw.

BUTTON BAND

With RS facing you, beg at neck edge, PU 88 (88, 92, 94, 96) sts along left front edge. Knit 5 rows. BO kw on WS.

BUTTONHOLE BAND

With RS facing you, beg at bottom edge, PU 88 (88, 92, 94, 96) sts along right front edge. Work buttonhole band as follows:

Row 1 (WS): Knit.

Row 2: K3, BO 3 sts, K12, BO 3 sts, K67 (67, 71, 73, 75).

Row 3: K67 (67, 71, 73, 75), CO 3 sts, K12, CO 3 sts, K3.

Row 4: Knit.

Row 5: BO kw on WS.

FINISHING

Sew buttons on left front edge to correspond to buttonholes. Weave in loose ends. Block if necessary.

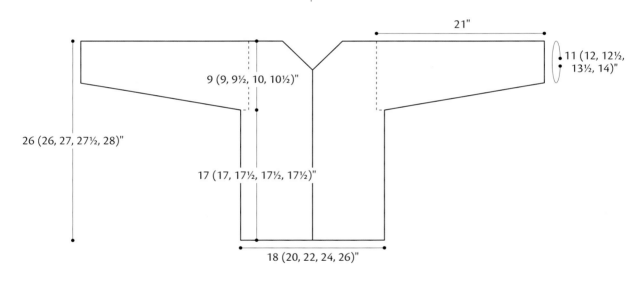

21"

9 (9, 9½, 10, 10½)"

11 (12, 12½, 13½, 14)"

26 (26, 27, 27½, 28)"

17 (17, 17½, 17½, 17½)"

18 (20, 22, 24, 26)"

CASUAL LIVING PULLOVER

The relaxed fit of this pullover, done in one piece from the bottom to the armholes, makes this sweater one that you will truly live in! Slightly flared styling and detail at the neckline, sleeve, and bottom bands make this a stylish sweater indeed.

Skill Level: Easy ◖■☐▷

Finished Bust Measurement: 37 (41, 45, 49, 53)"

Finished Length: 26 (26½, 27, 27½, 28)"

Sleeve Drop: 8½ (9, 9, 9½, 10)"

MATERIALS

Yarn: 6 (7, 8, 9, 10) skeins of Cotton Blossom Yarn from Farmhouse Yarns LLC (85% cotton, 15% rayon; 4 oz/125 g; 200 yds/182 m) in color Indigo, or approx 1200 (1350, 1500, 1700, 1950) yds of medium (worsted-weight) yarn 🧶**4**

Needles: Size 6 (4 mm) circular needles (16" and 29" long) or size required to attain gauge, size 6 double-pointed needles

Notions: Stitch markers, stitch holders

Gauge: 18 sts and 24 rows = 4" in St st

BODY

Beg at bottom and with 29" circular needle, CO 178 (196, 214, 232, 250) sts. Join, being careful not to twist, and pm to denote beg of rnd.

Purl 3 rnds.

Knit 6 rnds.

Purl 3 rnds.

Knit 6 rnds.

Purl 3 rnds.

Work in St st (knit every rnd) until piece measures 5 (5, 6, 6, 7)" from CO edge.

First dec rnd: *K20 (23, 26, 29, 32), K2tog, K45 (48, 51, 54, 57), K2tog, K20 (23, 26, 29, 32), rep from * once—174 (192, 210, 228, 246) total sts.

Work even in St st to 9 (9, 11, 11, 12)" from CO edge.

Second dec rnd: *K19 (22, 25, 28, 31), K2tog, K45 (48, 51, 54, 57), K2tog, K19 (22, 25, 28, 31), rep from * once—170 (188, 206, 224, 242) total sts.

Work even in St st to 13 (13, 15, 15, 16)" from CO edge.

Third dec rnd: *K18 (21, 24, 27, 30), K2tog, K45 (48, 51, 54, 57), K2tog, K18 (21, 24, 27, 30), rep from * once—166 (184, 202, 220, 238) total sts.

Work even until piece measures 17½ (17½, 18, 18, 18)" from CO edge or desired length to armhole.

Divide for front and back: K7 (9, 9, 11, 13), place previous 14 (18, 18, 22, 26) sts on holder for underarm gusset, K69 (74, 83, 88, 93), place these sts on holder for front, K14 (18, 18, 22, 26), place these sts on holder for 2nd underarm gusset, knit to end of rnd.

BACK

Working back and forth on rem 69 (74, 83, 88, 93) sts, cont in St st (knit RS rows, purl WS rows) until back measures 7½ (8, 8, 8½, 9)" from dividing row, ending with WS row.

Neck shaping: K23 (25, 29, 31, 33), place center 23 (24, 25, 26, 27) sts on holder for neckband, attach 2nd skein of yarn and knit rem 23 (25, 29, 31, 33) sts.

Work both sides at the same time in St st until armhole measures 8½ (9, 9, 9½, 10)". Place sts on holders for shoulders.

FRONT

Return 69 (74, 83, 88, 93) front sts to working needle. With RS facing you, attach yarn and work even in St st until piece measures 2½ (3, 3, 3½, 4)" from dividing row, ending with WS row.

Neck shaping: K28 (30, 34, 36, 38), place center 13 (14, 15, 16, 17) sts on holder, attach 2nd skein of yarn and knit rem 28 (30, 34, 36, 38) sts.

Working both sides at the same time from separate skeins of yarn, work in St st, dec 1 st at each side of neck every RS row a total of 5 times.

Recommended dec: K2tog on left front edge, ssk on right front edge.

Work even on rem 23 (25, 29, 31, 33) sts until front is same length as back, ending with WS row. Join front and back shoulder sections using 3-needle BO (page 76).

SLEEVES

With RS facing you, sl 14 (18, 18, 22, 26) sts from underarm holder to 16" circular needle, pm, PU 82 (86, 90, 94, 96) sts around armhole opening, pm—96 (104, 108, 116, 122) total sts.

K7 (9, 9, 11, 13) underarm sts and pm (use different color) to denote beg of rnd.

Rnd 1: Knit.

Rnd 2: Sl beg-of-rnd marker, knit to 2 sts before marker, K2tog, sm, knit to next marker, sm, ssk, knit to end of rnd.

Rep rnds 1 and 2 until 1 st rem between markers. Remove markers except at beg of rnd—84 (88, 92, 96, 98) sts.

Cont in St st, dec 1 st at beg and end of every 4 rnds until 48 (48, 54, 54, 60) sts rem.

Work even until sleeve measures 17" from PU row or 3" less than desired finished sleeve length, switching to dpns when too few sts for circular needle.

Sleeve Border

Purl 3 rounds.

Knit 3 rounds.

Purl 3 rounds.

Knit 3 rounds.

Purl 2 rounds.

BO pw.

NECKBAND

With RS facing you and 16" circular needle, beg at left front shoulder, PU 28 sts along left front neck edge, K13 (14, 15, 16, 17) from front neck holder, PU 28 sts along right front neck edge, PU 5 sts along right back neck edge, K23 (24, 25, 26, 27) from back neck holder, PU 5 sts along left back neck edge—102 (104, 106, 108, 110) total sts. Pm to denote beg of rnd.

Work neckband as follows:

Purl 3 rnds.

Knit 3 rnds.

Purl 3 rnds.

Knit 3 rnds.

Purl 2 rnds.

BO pw.

FINISHING

Weave in all loose ends. Block.

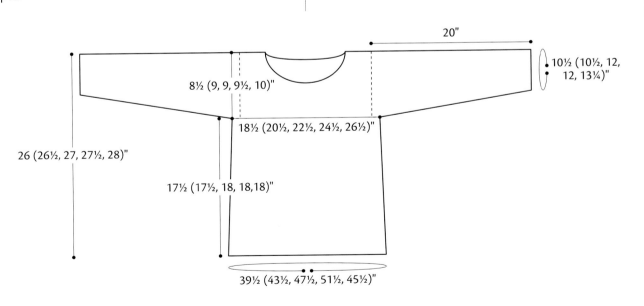

20"

10½ (10½, 12, 12, 13¼)"

8½ (9, 9, 9½, 10)"

18½ (20½, 22½, 24½, 26½)"

26 (26½, 27, 27½, 28)"

17½ (17½, 18, 18,18)"

39½ (43½, 47½, 51½, 45½)"

GARTER AND I-CORD PULLOVER

For this garter-stitch pullover, the construction process is anything but ordinary, yet it's oh-so-simple. Made from rectangular panels with no increases or decreases, this comfy pullover is trimmed with applied I-cord and has no seams to sew.

Skill Level: Intermediate ◖■■▭

Finished Bust Measurement:	36 (40, 44, 48, 52)"
Finished Length:	22½ (22½, 23½, 23½, 24½)"
Sleeve Drop:	9 (9, 9½, 9½, 10)"
Sleeve Length:	20 (20, 20, 20, 20)"

MATERIALS

Yarn: 7 (8, 9, 10, 11) hanks of Highlander by Alpaca with a Twist (45% baby alpaca, 45% merino wool, 2% viscose; 3.5 oz/100 g; 145 yds/132 m) in color 3014, or approx 1015 (1160, 1305, 1450, 1595) yds of medium (worsted-weight) yarn (4)

Needles: Size 8 (5 mm) circular needles (16" and 29" or longer) or size required to attain gauge, size 8 needles, size 8 double-pointed needles

Notions: Stitch holders, spare needles (smaller than size 8)

Gauge: 16 sts and 22 rows = 4" in garter stitch

SIDE PANELS (MAKE 2)

Each side panel is one continuous piece, starting at bottom front and extending up over shoulder to bottom back. Length of panel is actually twice the finished length of sweater.

With straight needles, CO 21 (23, 23, 25, 25) sts.

All rows: Knit to last 3 sts, wyif sl 3 sts pw. Pm to denote this side as RS.

Work until piece measures 44 (46, 46, 48, 48)", ending with RS row. BO on WS.

CENTER BACK PANEL

With RS facing you, beg at lower right edge of side panel, using long circular needle, PU 84 (88, 88, 92, 92) sts along outermost edge of I-cord trim.

Next row: Knit back on these sts.

PICK-UP HINT!

Because I-cord is a tube, when you pick up stitches on the outermost edge it's actually along the "bar," before the first stitch of I-cord on the row. It will appear that you're picking up stitches on the wrong side. Doing it this way makes the I-cord pop out more.

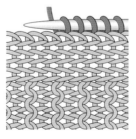

Right side

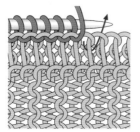

Wrong side

Beg back panel as follows:

Row 1 (RS): Knit to last 3 sts, wyib sl 3 sts as if to purl.

Row 2: P3, knit to end of row.

Rep these 2 rows until center back panel measures 5 (5, 6, 6, 6)", ending with WS row. By slipping last 3 sts on RS rows and purling them on WS rows, you're forming a rolled I-cord edging along neckline as back section is knit.

Joining Right Side Panel

Join back panel to right side panel using 3-needle BO (page 76) as follows: Hold side panel and back RS tog. PU "bar" (inside loop) before first I-cord st and place on LH needle. Knit this st tog with first "live" stitch on back section. *Knit next bar and live st tog. BO first st over second st, rep from * to end.

RIGHT UNDERARM PANEL

Pm on right side panel 13½ (13½, 14, 14, 14½)" from bottom edge. With RS of sweater back facing you, beg at lower outside edge of right side panel and ending at marker, PU 54 (54, 56, 56, 58) sts along outermost edge of I-cord.

Next row: Knit.

Work as for center panel until piece measures 3 (4, 5, 6, 7)" from PU row, ending with RS row. Join to front right side panel using 3-needle BO as for joining back section.

Rep for left underarm panel.

CENTER FRONT

With RS facing you, beg at lower edge of right side panel using longer circular needle, PU 66 (70, 70, 74, 74) sts along outermost edge of I-cord trim.

Next row: Knit back on PU sts. Beg front panel as follows:

Row 1 (RS): Knit to last 3 sts, wyib sl 3 sts pw.

Row 2: P3, knit to end of row.

Rep rows 1 and 2 until center front panel measures 5 (5, 6, 6, 6)", ending with WS row.

Join to side panel on left front using same technique as for back section. Join front section to left-side panel using 3-needle BO as for back section.

SLEEVES

With RS facing you, locate center of underarm section. Beg 1 st from right of center using 16" circular needle, PU 87 (91, 99, 103, 111) sts as follows: PU 3 (3, 3, 3, 3) sts for I-cord, pm, PU 6 (8, 10, 12, 14) sts along rem left side of underarm section, pm, PU 72 (72, 76, 76, 80) sts around armhole opening, pm, PU 6 (8, 10, 12, 14) sts along right side of underarm section, pm (use a different color) to denote beg of rnd.

Gusset Shaping

Rnd 1 and all odd-numbered rnds: Wyib sl 3 sts pw, purl to end of rnd, sl markers as you come to them.

Rnd 2: K3, sm, K4 (6, 8, 10, 12), K2tog, knit to last 6 (8, 10, 12, 14) sts, K2tog, knit to end of rnd.

Rnd 4: K3, sm, K3 (5, 7, 9, 11), K2tog, knit to last 5 (7, 9, 11, 13) sts, K2tog, knit to end of rnd.

Rnd 6: K3, sm, K2 (4, 6, 8, 10), K2tog, knit to last 4 (6, 8, 10, 12) sts, K2tog, knit to end of rnd.

Cont dec as estab, having 1 less st on each side of underarm section between decs until 5 (5, 5, 5, 5) sts rem in underarm section, including 3 I-cord sts, ending with dec rnd. Remove all markers except beg-of-rnd marker.

Sleeve Body

Rnd 1: Knit.

Rnd 2: Wyib sl 3 sts pw, purl to end of round.

Work even in patt on rem 77 (77, 81, 81, 85) sts until sleeve measures 4 (4, 4½, 5, 5½)" from PU row at armhole.

ATTACHED I-CORD TRIM

Taking the I-cord technique one step further is attached I-cord. This makes a wonderful edging to use on sweaters, blankets, and much more.

You must have live stitches to work from. If you don't, then you need to pick up stitches around the outside edge of the garment where you want to put the I-cord trim. Use a needle the same size as your project needles and pick up the stitches with the right side of the work facing you.

After you pick up the last required stitch, break yarn. Using a different needle, cast on three stitches (this number can be altered to make either a wider or narrower cord). Slip these stitches onto the end of the needle with the picked-up stitches.

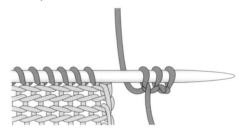

Cast on 3 stitches and slip them
to the other needle.

With the right side of the work facing you, knit two stitches (or one stitch less than the number of stitches you cast on), knit two together (using the last stitch from the stitches you cast on and the next stitch from those you picked up). Return the stitches that are now on the right-hand needle back to the left-hand needle and repeat the procedure. Keep repeating until you have used all the stitches picked up from the garment edge. Bind off.

Note: If you need to go around a corner while applying the I-cord, you may work an extra row or two of I-cord without attaching it so the trim lies flat.

Cont in patt, dec 1 st each side of I-cord on next row and every 6 rows thereafter until 37 (41, 41, 45, 45) sts rem, ending with rnd 2. Switch to dpns when too few sts for circular needle.

Recommended dec: K2tog.

Work even until sleeve measures 20" or desired finished sleeve length.

CO 3 sts to LH needle and work applied I-cord trim around cuff (see page 76).

FINISHING

Beg at center back using longer circular needle, PU 152 (160, 168, 176, 184) sts around bottom edge of sweater. CO an additional 3 sts and work applied I-cord around entire bottom edge of sweater. Weave in all ends. Block sweater if necessary.

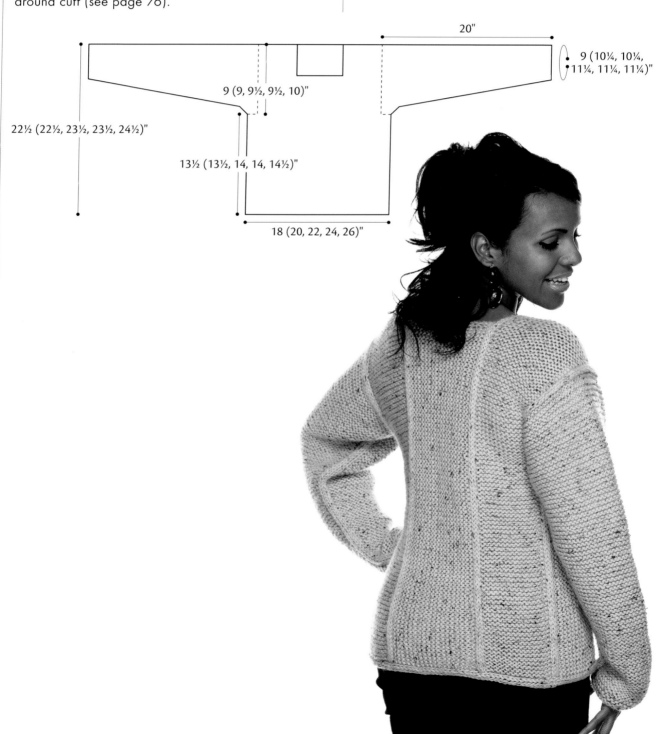

20"

9 (10¼, 10¼, 11¼, 11¼, 11¼)"

9 (9, 9½, 9½, 10)"

22½ (22½, 23½, 23½, 24½)"

13½ (13½, 14, 14, 14½)"

18 (20, 22, 24, 26)"

TECHNIQUES

Refer to the following instructions if you need help with general knitting techniques.

BASIC PATTERN STITCHES

Most of the designs in this book use the following basic pattern stitches.

Garter Stitch

In the round: Knit odd-numbered rounds; purl even-numbered rounds.

Back and forth: Knit every row.

Stockinette Stitch

In the round: Knit every round.

Back and forth: Knit right-side rows; purl wrong-side rows.

CASTING ON

There are endless ways to cast on; usually it doesn't make a difference what type of cast on you do. You can simply go with your favorite. However, there are times when a particular cast on is required for proper garment construction as well as final appearance. Following are the specific cast ons used for the designs in this book.

Provisional Cast On

The provisional cast on is a form of invisibly casting on. This technique is used when you need to work the cast-on stitches at a later point in the garment construction, creating an invisible join.

Pick a piece of even-textured scrap yarn and a crochet hook that is the appropriate size for the yarn you will be knitting with. Crochet a chain that contains approximately 10% more stitches than you need to cast on (that is, if the pattern says to provisionally cast on 50 stitches, make a chain of approximately 55 stitches). Don't worry if your chain isn't perfect; you

will be ripping it out at a later point in the construction of the garment anyway.

Once you have the number of stitches required, cut the yarn and pull the tail through the last loop to secure. Take a look at your chain. You'll notice that the front side has V shapes, while the back side has horizontal bars.

With the yarn and needles required for the garment, pick up stitches through the bar on the back side of the chain. To easily do this, insert the needle from the top down into the bar, wrap the working yarn around the needle, and pull through a stitch.

Don't worry if you miss a bar along the way. That's why you made the chain longer than you needed!

To remove the chain, simply take out the securing end of the chain (the end of the chain where you stopped making stitches) and place the stitches back on a knitting needle. To keep the stitches from getting twisted during the process, be sure that the right-hand side of each stitch is toward the front of the needle.

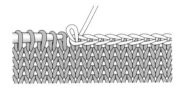

Knitted Cast On

The knitted cast on is great for casting on stitches in the middle of a row. It's also useful when you need to cast on a large number of stitches (for an afghan or sweater knit in the round, for example). You don't have to guess the amount of yarn that will be needed on the "tail" end of the cast-on yarn. Some people, however, have a tendency to make the knitted cast on too tight, so be careful of this.

Make a slipknot and place it on the needle in your left hand. Knit that stitch, but do not take it off of either needle. Now, bring the left-hand needle around to the front, pick up the stitch (going from the bottom of the stitch) that was created on the right-hand needle, and place it on the left-hand needle.

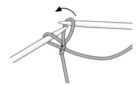

Knit into first stitch. Leave stitch on needle.

Slip the stitch on the right needle to the left needle.

Tighten slightly around the needle. Repeat this process until you reach the needed number of stitches.

INCREASING

While there are numerous methods of increasing stitches, the following are the recommended methods for the designs in this book.

Knit in Front and Back of Stitch (K1f&b)

This stitch is one of the most basic and easiest ways to increase. You simply knit into the stitch you want to increase in as you normally would, only don't take the stitch off of either needle.

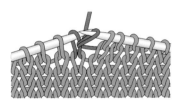

Now, bring the right needle around to the back of your work and knit that same stitch again, this time going into the back loop of the stitch you are increasing in.

Be aware that this type of increase will result in one normal-looking stitch while the other stitch will have a horizontal bar going across it. You didn't do anything wrong. That is just how this increase looks. Usually this little bar doesn't cause any problems, but on occasion it does take away from the look of the garment, and you may want to opt for a different increase method.

Make One (M1)

Another way to increase stitches is to work a "make one" increase. When correctly done, this increase is virtually invisible.

Work up to the point where the increase is supposed to go. Pick up the horizontal bar between the stitch just worked and the next stitch by inserting the left needle from front to back and placing the acquired loop on the left needle. Now, you'll simply knit this stitch through the back loop.

You'll notice that you are actually twisting the stitch as you knit it. If you don't twist the stitch, you'll get a hole where the bar was picked up. By knitting into the back of the stitch, you'll eliminate the hole.

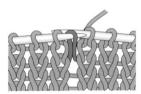

Pick up the horizontal bar.

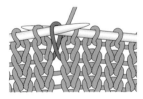

Knit into the back of the stitch.

Lifted Increase (L1)

This increase is virtually invisible. It's done by pulling up a loop from the row below the one you are currently working on.

Work to where the increase is to be. Insert the left needle into the right half of the stitch in the row below the next stitch on the left needle, going from front to back. Knit this stitch. Now knit the stitch that is on the left needle. You have created two stitches from one.

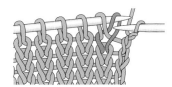

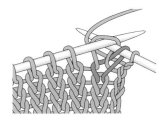

DECREASING

While there are many ways to decrease, the following are methods that were most often used for the garments in this book.

Knit Two Together (K2tog)

This is a right-slanting decrease. When completed, the stitch will slant toward the right. Instead of knitting the next stitch on the left needle, simply insert the right-hand needle from left to right through both the second stitch and the first stitch on the left-hand needle. Knit them as one stitch.

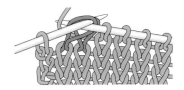

Slip, Slip, Knit (ssk)

The slip, slip, knit is a left-slanting decrease. When completed, the stitch will slant to the left. It's a mirror image of the knit-two-together decrease. Work to where the decrease is to be made. Slip the next two stitches *individually*, as if to knit, to the right-hand needle.

Insert your left-hand needle into the front part of these stitches, from top to bottom, and knit these two stitches together, making one stitch.

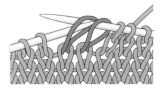

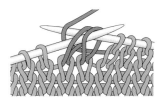

PICKING UP STITCHES

To pick up stitches, insert the needle under both strands of the existing edge stitch. If you go through only the very outside loop, then the stitch is pulled and contorted. By going through both strands, the stitch stays even and there are no holes. Should a particular stitch appear loose or leave a hole, you can knit this stitch through the back loop and that should take care of it!

Picked-up stitches need to be evenly spaced. Since the number of stitches per row isn't the same as stitches per inch, you may have to make some adjustments when picking up stitches. You don't need to pick up a stitch in every space across. Just pick them up evenly so as not to have any holes.

To pick up stitches for the neckband, I find it easiest to divide the neck opening into equal sections. Divide the number of stitches to be picked up by the number of sections. Pick up that number of stitches in each section. This assures the stitches are evenly spaced around the neckband.

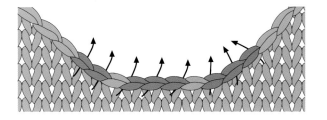

I-CORD

I-cord is a wonderful way to make drawstrings and ties for your knitted items. While it may seem a little awkward to do at first, once you get the hang of it, you'll be able to do it in your sleep!

The width of I-cord is determined by the number of cast-on stitches and the weight of yarn you are using. Four stitches is usually a good number to start with.

Using double-pointed needles in the same size as you used for the body of the sweater (unless the pattern specifies differently), cast on four stitches (or the number specified in the pattern). Knit these stitches. *Do not turn work.* Place the needle with the stitches in your left hand and slide the stitches back to the opposite end of the needle. Knit these four stitches again, making sure the yarn is pulled snugly when it's brought from the last stitch worked in the previous row to the first stitch worked in this row. *Do not turn work.* Continue to slide the stitches to the opposite end of the needle and knit them. The yarn is pulled across the back each time to start the new row. After three to four rows, you'll see a cord being formed.

If the cord is loose, it's most likely because the yarn isn't pulled tightly across the back when beginning each row.

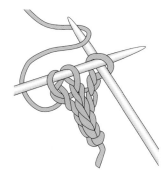

ASSEMBLY

How a sweater is sewn together can "make or break" the entire garment. Sometimes it takes trial and error to decide which method of assembly is best for each instance. You definitely don't want to rush through the finishing part. You may find a different method that works better for you, but here is what works best for me.

Flat Sleeve Assembly

This technique works great for sewing sleeves that were knit flat to a body section that was also knit flat. Measure from the shoulder down on both the front and back sections the depth of the sleeve (as given in the beginning of the pattern directions) and place markers. Now find the center point of the sleeve and place a marker there.

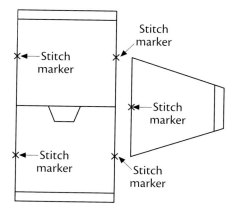

Place the right side of the sleeve together with the right side of the body, matching up the shoulder seam with the center sleeve marker and the sleeve edges with the markers you placed for sleeve depth.

Thread a piece of yarn (or use the tail left from the bind off of the sleeve if you remembered to leave a long enough one) on a tapestry needle. Attach the sleeve to the body by weaving back and forth. It's essential to maintain an even tension so your seam doesn't pucker or leave holes. I find it works best to go through both layers of the bound-off stitch on the sleeve and the very outside loop of the stitch on the body. This will make a nice, flat seam. My golden rule is that you must go through each and every bound-off stitch of the sleeve, but you don't have to go through every stitch on the body sections. Simply line up the sleeve section and go through the stitch on the body that is directly across from it. You should find, however, that you will only be skipping an occasional stitch.

Three-Needle Bind Off

This is a very attractive bind off that adds stability to the shoulder area. Place the back shoulder stitches and front shoulder stitches on separate needles, the same size you used to knit your sweater. Hold these needles in your left hand with the right sides of the knitting together.

With a third needle (the same size), knit the first stitch from the front needle together with the first stitch from the back needle, ending up with one stitch on the right-hand needle. Knit the next two stitches together in the same manner, ending up with two stitches on the right-hand needle. Bring the first stitch you knit up and over the second stitch you knit to bind off one stitch.

Continue working across the row, knitting one stitch from the front together with one stitch from the back. Each time you have two stitches on the right-hand needle, bind one off. When you get down to one stitch, cut the yarn and pull the tail through the remaining stitch to secure your work.

Knit together 1 stitch from front needle and 1 stitch from back needle.

Bind off.

Kitchener Stitch

The Kitchener stitch is a type of grafting used to join two pieces of knitting together. It's done by creating a row of knitting by hand with a tapestry needle and is completely flat and invisible when correctly done.

For the projects in this book, you'll remove the provisional chain and place the live stitches on a knitting needle the same size as your project needles. Each set of stitches from the front and the back go on separate needles.

Hold the needles together in your left hand with the wrong sides of the work together. Thread on a tapestry needle a piece of yarn long enough to work the number of stitches you have on the needles. Make sure you have enough yarn so you don't run out partway through.

First Stitch
Front needle: Insert the tapestry needle as if to purl that stitch, leave the stitch on the knitting needle, and pull the yarn through.

Back needle: Insert the tapestry needle as if to knit that stitch, leave the stitch on the knitting needle, and pull the yarn through.

Remainder of Row to Last Stitch
Front needle: Insert the tapestry needle as if to knit the first stitch and slip it off the knitting needle onto the tapestry needle. Immediately go through the next stitch on the front needle as if to purl, leaving it on the knitting needle, and pull the yarn through.

Back needle: Insert the tapestry needle as if to purl the first stitch and slip it off the knitting needle onto the tapestry needle. Immediately go through the next stitch on the back needle as if to knit, leaving it on the knitting needle, and pull the yarn through.

Last Stitch
Front needle: Insert the tapestry needle as if to knit the stitch and slip it off the knitting needle.

Back needle: Insert the tapestry needle as if to purl the stitch, slip it off the knitting needle, and pull the yarn through.

Weave in the yarn tail on the wrong side.

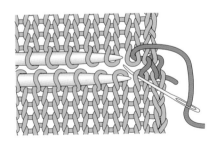

ABBREVIATIONS

approx	approximately
beg	begin(ning)
BO	bind off
CC	contrasting color
CO	cast on
cont	continue, continuing
dec(s)	decrease(s), decreasing
dpn(s)	double-pointed needle(s)
estab	established
foll	following
g	grams
inc(s)	increase(s), increasing
K	knit
K1f&b	knit into the front and back of next stitch (1 stitch increased)
K2tog	knit 2 stitches together (1 stitch decreased)
kw	knitwise
L1	lifted increase (see page 74)
M1	make 1 stitch (see page 74)
MC	main color
oz	ounces
P	purl
patt	pattern
pm	place marker
psso	slip 1 stitch, knit 1 stitch, and then pass slipped stitch over knit stitch (1 stitch decreased)

PU	pick up and knit
pw	purlwise
rem	remain(s)(ing)
rep(s)	repeat(s)
rnd(s)	round(s)
RS	right side
sl	slip
sl 1 pw-K1-YO-psso	slip 1 stitch purlwise, yarn over, pass slipped stitch over
sl 1-K2tog-psso	slip 1 stitch, knit 2 stitches together, pass slipped stitch over
sm	slip marker
ssk	slip 2 stitches individually as if to knit, then knit these 2 stitches together (1 stitch decreased)
st(s)	stitch(es)
St st	stockinette stitch
tbl	through back loop
tog	together
WS	wrong side
wyib	with yarn in back
wyif	with yarn in front
yd(s)	yard(s)
YO	yarn over

USEFUL INFORMATION

STANDARD YARN-WEIGHT SYSTEM

In this book, project yarns are labeled with yarn-weight categories compiled by the Craft Yarn Council of America. Refer to the following chart for descriptions of the various categories.

STANDARD YARN WEIGHTS							
Yarn-Weight Symbol and Category Name	**0** Lace	**1** Super Fine	**2** Fine	**3** Light	**4** Medium	**5** Bulky	**6** Super Bulky
Types of Yarn in Category	Fingering, 10-count crochet thread	Sock, Fingering, Baby	Sport, Baby	DK, Light worsted	Worsted, Afghan, Aran	Chunky, Craft, Rug	Bulky, Roving
Knit Gauge Range* in Stockinette Stitch to 4"	33 to 40** sts	27 to 32 sts	23 to 26 sts	21 to 24 sts	16 to 20 sts	12 to 15 sts	6 to 11 sts
Recommended Needle in Metric Size Range	1.5 to 2.25 mm	2.25 to 3.25 mm	3.25 to 3.75 mm	3.75 to 4.5 mm	4.5 to 5.5 mm	5.5 to 8 mm	8 mm and larger
Recommended Needle in U.S. Size Range	000 to 1	1 to 3	3 to 5	5 to 7	7 to 9	9 to 11	11 and larger

*These are guidelines only. The above ranges reflect the most commonly used gauges and needle or hook sizes for specific yarn categories. Always follow the gauge stated in your pattern.

**Lace-weight yarns are usually knit or crocheted on larger needles and hooks to create lacy, openwork patterns. Accordingly, a gauge range is difficult to determine.

SKILL-LEVEL LIST

The projects in this book are rated using the following guidelines created by the Craft Yarn Council of America.

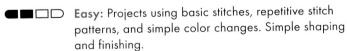

Beginner: Projects for first-time knitters using basic knit and purl stitches. Minimal shaping.

Easy: Projects using basic stitches, repetitive stitch patterns, and simple color changes. Simple shaping and finishing.

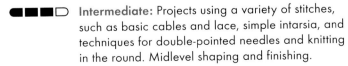

Intermediate: Projects using a variety of stitches, such as basic cables and lace, simple intarsia, and techniques for double-pointed needles and knitting in the round. Midlevel shaping and finishing.

Experienced: Projects using advanced techniques and stitches, such as short rows, Fair Isle, more intricate intarsia, cables, lace patterns, and numerous color changes.

METRIC CONVERSION CHART

METRIC CONVERSION CHART				
m	=	yds	x	0.9144
yds	=	m	x	1.0936
g	=	oz	x	28.35
oz	=	g	x	0.0352

RESOURCES

The following companies have supplied yarns and/or buttons for this book. Their generosity is greatly appreciated. For a list of shops in your area that carry the products mentioned in this book, please contact these companies.

Alpaca with a Twist
950 S. White River Pkwy W Dr
Indianapolis, IN 46221
www.alpacawithatwist.com

Araucania Yarns
Knitting Fever, Inc.
35 Debevoise Ave
Roosevelt, NY 11575-0502
www.knittingfever.com

Buttons, Etc.
2 Heitz Pl
Hicksville, NY 11801
www.buttonsetc.com

Cascade Yarns
PO Box 58168
Tukwila, WA 98138-1168
www.cascadeyarns.com

Claudia Hand Painted Yarns
40 W Washington St
Harrisonburg, VA 22802
www.claudiaco.com

DiVe Yarns
Cascade Yarns
PO Box 58168
Tukwila, WA 98138-1168
www.cascadeyarns.com

Dill Button
616 Kaiser Hollow Rd
Montoursville, PA 17754-9639
www.dill-buttons.com

Farmhouse Yarns
283 Mount Parnassus Rd
East Haddam, CT 06423
www.farmhouseyarns.com

Euroyarns
Knitting Fever, Inc.
35 Debevoise Ave
Roosevelt, NY 11575-0502
www.knittingfever.com

Happy Hands Yarns
www.happyhandsyarn.com

Interlacements
PO Box 3082
Colorado Springs, CO 80934-3082
www.interlacementsyarns.com

Louet Yarns
3425 Hands Rd
Prescott, Ontario K0E 1T0
Canada
www.louet.com

Mirasol Yarns
Knitting Fever, Inc.
35 Debevoise Ave
Roosevelt, NY 11575-0502
www.knittingfever.com

Noro Yarns
Knitting Fever, Inc.
35 Debevoise Ave
Roosevelt, NY 11575-0502
www.knittingfever.com

Queensland Collection
Knitting Fever, Inc.
35 Debevoise Ave
Roosevelt, NY 11575-0502
www.knittingfever.com

Schulana Yarns
Skacel Collection, Inc.
PO Box 88110
Seattle, WA 98138
www.skacelknitting.com

Sirdar
Knitting Fever, Inc.
35 Debevoise Ave
Roosevelt, NY 11575-0502
www.knittingfever.com

Zitron Yarns
Skacel Collection, Inc.
PO Box 88110
Seattle, WA 98138
www.skacelknitting.com